GRAPHIC FORENSIC SCIENCE

DETECTIVE WORK WITH BALLISTICS

by David West

illustrated by Emanuele Boccanfuso

rosen publishing's
rosen central

New York

Published in 2008 by The Rosen Publishing Group, Inc.
29 East 21st Street, New York, NY 10010

First edition, 2008

Designed and produced by
David West Books

Editor: Gail Bushnell

Photo credits:
4-5, Stefan Klein.

   Library of Congress Cataloging-in-Publication Data

West, David, 1956-
   Detective work with ballistics / by David West ; illustrated by
Emanuele Boccanfuso. -- 1st ed.
      p. cm. -- (Graphic forensic science)
   Includes index.
   ISBN 978-1-4042-1434-7 (library binding) -- ISBN 978-1-4042-1435-4 (pbk.) --
   ISBN 978-1-4042-1436-1 (6 pack)
   1. Bullets--Identification. 2. Forensic ballistics. I. Title.
   HV8077.W47 2007
   363.25'62--dc22

                                        2007045212

Manufactured in China

CONTENTS

SOLVING A CRIME

When a serious crime has been committed, such as murder, evidence needs to be collected at the scene of the crime and examined carefully.

The Evidence

Once a crime scene has been discovered, it is cordoned off while crime scene investigators (CSI) carry out a detailed examination of the site. As well as gathering evidence, they make a detailed record of the scene by taking photographs, and making sketches. The evidence is then taken to a crime laboratory, where specialist experts, called forensic scientists, examine it. They perform tests, from firing suspect guns to taking DNA samples from blood collected at the crime scene. The evidence may also be compared to archived material such as ballistic reports, fingerprint files, or dental records, as well as being downloaded onto computerized archives for future use.

Gradually, a file of evidence is created that can be used by the police to help locate and arrest a criminal. The evidence is also used in a court of law to convict the criminal.

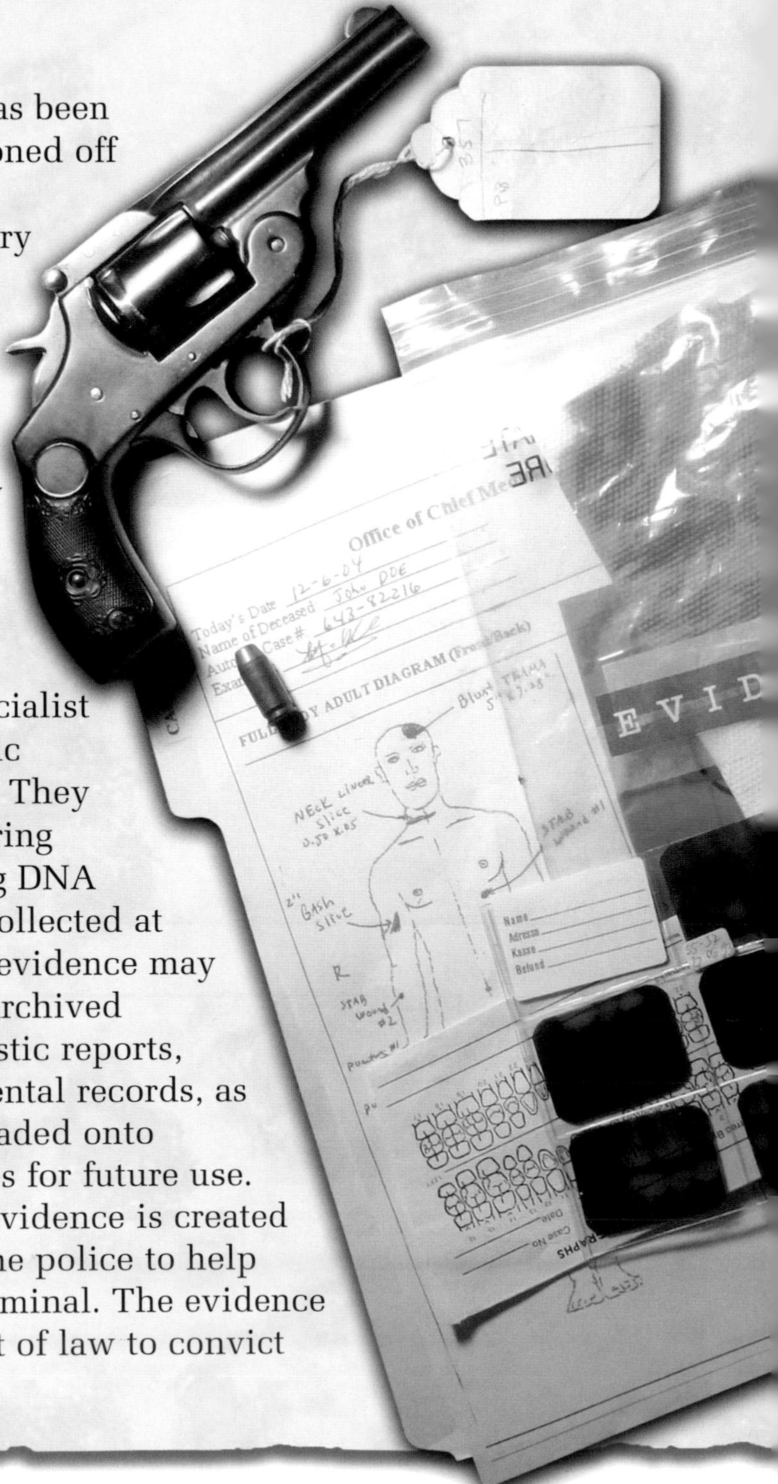

Office of Chief Me
Today's Date 12-6-04
Name of Deceased John DOE
FULL BODY ADULT DIAGRAM
E V I D
Name
Adresse
Kasse
Befund

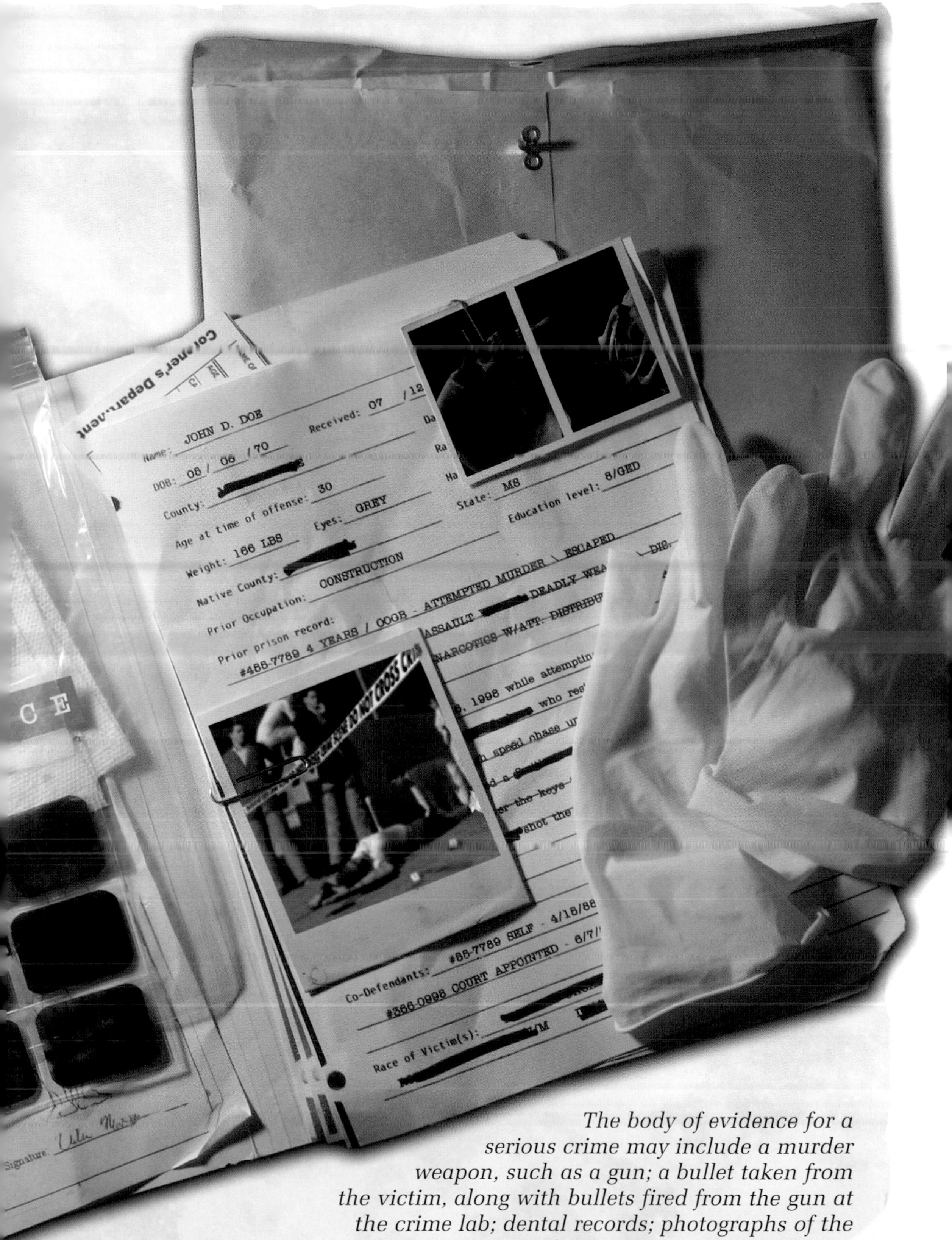
Coroner's Department
Name: JOHN D. DOE
Received: 07 / 12
DOB: 08 / 08 / 70
County: [redacted]
Age at time of offense: 30
State: MS
Eyes: GREY
Education level: 8/GED
Weight: 166 LBS
Native County: [redacted]
Prior Occupation: CONSTRUCTION
Prior prison record:
#466-7789 4 YEARS / OOGB - ATTEMPTED MURDER \ ESCAPED
DO NOT CROSS CRIME
Co-Defendants: #86-7789 SELF - 4/16/88
#366-0998 COURT APPOINTED
Race of Victim(s): [redacted] /M
Signature

The body of evidence for a serious crime may include a murder weapon, such as a gun; a bullet taken from the victim, along with bullets fired from the gun at the crime lab; dental records; photographs of the crime scene, along with sketches; witnesses' statements; and a pathologist's report.

THE FORENSIC BALLISTICS EXPERT

Forensic ballistics is the science of analyzing guns and bullets used in crimes.

BULLETS

The barrels of pistols and rifles have twisting grooves that spin the bullet, making it more accurate. On the bullet, they leave markings, called a ballistic fingerprint, which are individual to every gun. A gun can be proved to be a murder weapon by comparing bullets fired from it with those found in a murder victim.

Powder markings
Evidence from the exploding gunpowder may give clues as to how close a weapon was to the victim.

Bullet
Bullets fired from a handgun have unique markings made by the rifling inside the barrel.

This bullet shows marks made by rifling.

C. Goddard

MICROSCOPES

Working for Charles Waite, Philip Gravelle invented the comparison microscope in the 1920s. Investigators could now compare the markings on bullets and shells side by side. Waite cataloged test firings of every type of handgun. Today there is a huge archive that experts use to compare bullets fired from a firearm with bullets found at a crime scene. When Waite died in 1926, Calvin Goddard took over and became the world's foremost ballistics expert.

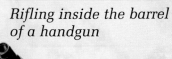

Rifling inside the barrel of a handgun

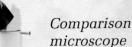

Comparison microscope

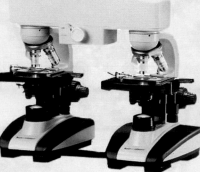

Cartridge case

As with the bullet, the cartridge case can leave ballistic fingerprints. The firing pin can leave an individual mark on the percussion cap, and minute marks can be made by the ejector and breechblock.

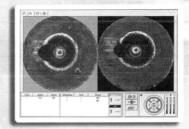

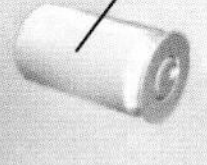

Firing-pin markings are compared on a computer database.

Breechblock traces ——

Ejector mark ——

Firing-pin mark

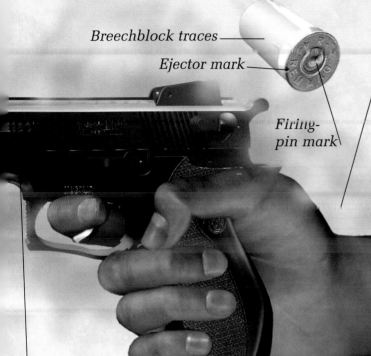

Powder markings 2

Every time a gun is fired, smoke and particles are ejected. Minute amounts land on the shooter's hand and clothing. These can show up when a swab is taken and examined in the lab.

Serial Numbers

Criminals often file off the serial number so that the gun cannot be traced to the buyer. Examiners can get the number to show up using a special method involving acid.

Laser light attached to a dowel

AT THE CRIME SCENE

Ballistics experts may also be called to the scene of a crime. Evidence such as powder burns from firearms, on the victim or on the suspect, can be used as evidence. Bullet holes in walls are measured and photographed. Special dowels with lasers are inserted into these holes to show where the bullets were fired from, helping investigators work out exactly what happened.

HENRY GODDARD AND THE FIRST BALLISTICS CASE

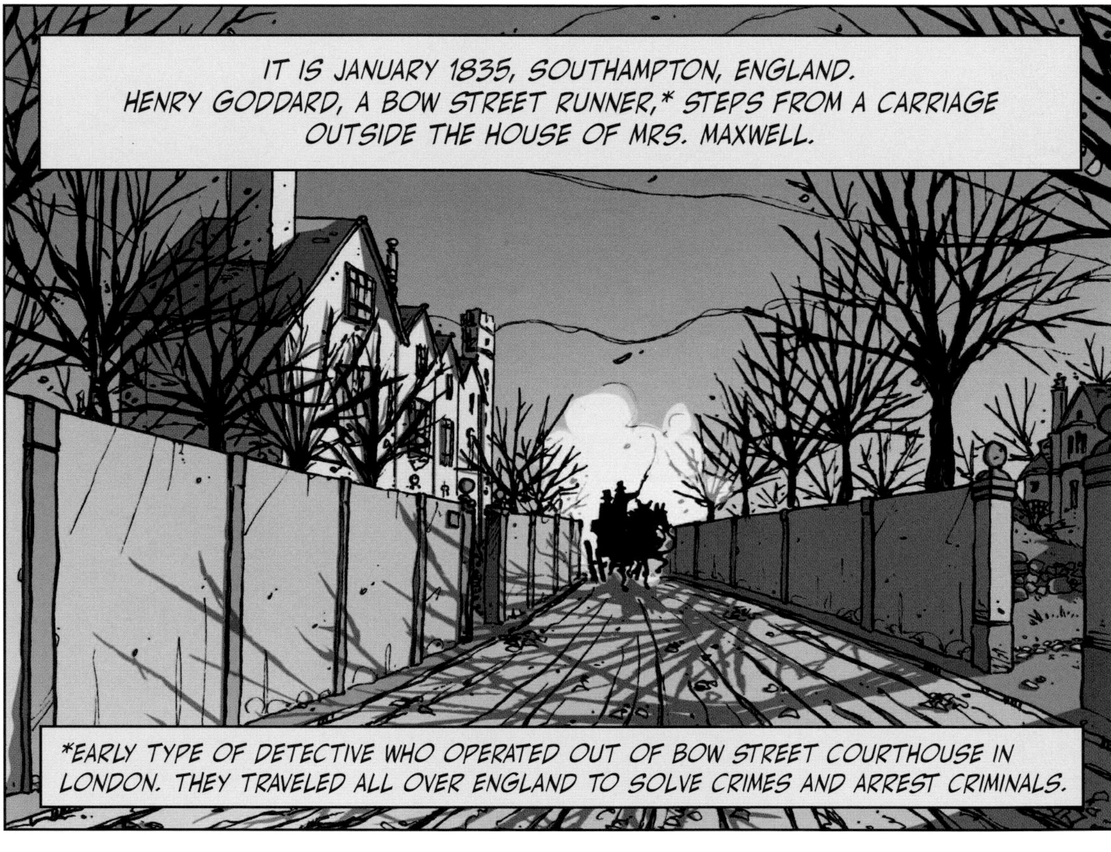
IT IS JANUARY 1835, SOUTHAMPTON, ENGLAND.
HENRY GODDARD, A BOW STREET RUNNER,* STEPS FROM A CARRIAGE OUTSIDE THE HOUSE OF MRS. MAXWELL.
*EARLY TYPE OF DETECTIVE WHO OPERATED OUT OF BOW STREET COURTHOUSE IN LONDON. THEY TRAVELED ALL OVER ENGLAND TO SOLVE CRIMES AND ARREST CRIMINALS.

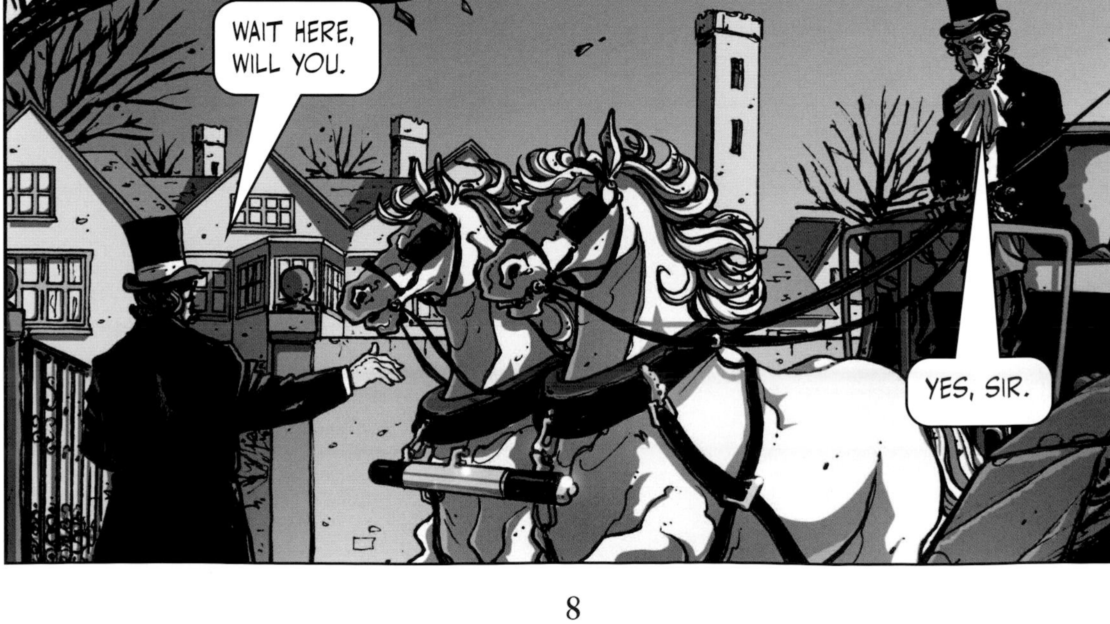
WAIT HERE, WILL YOU.
YES, SIR.

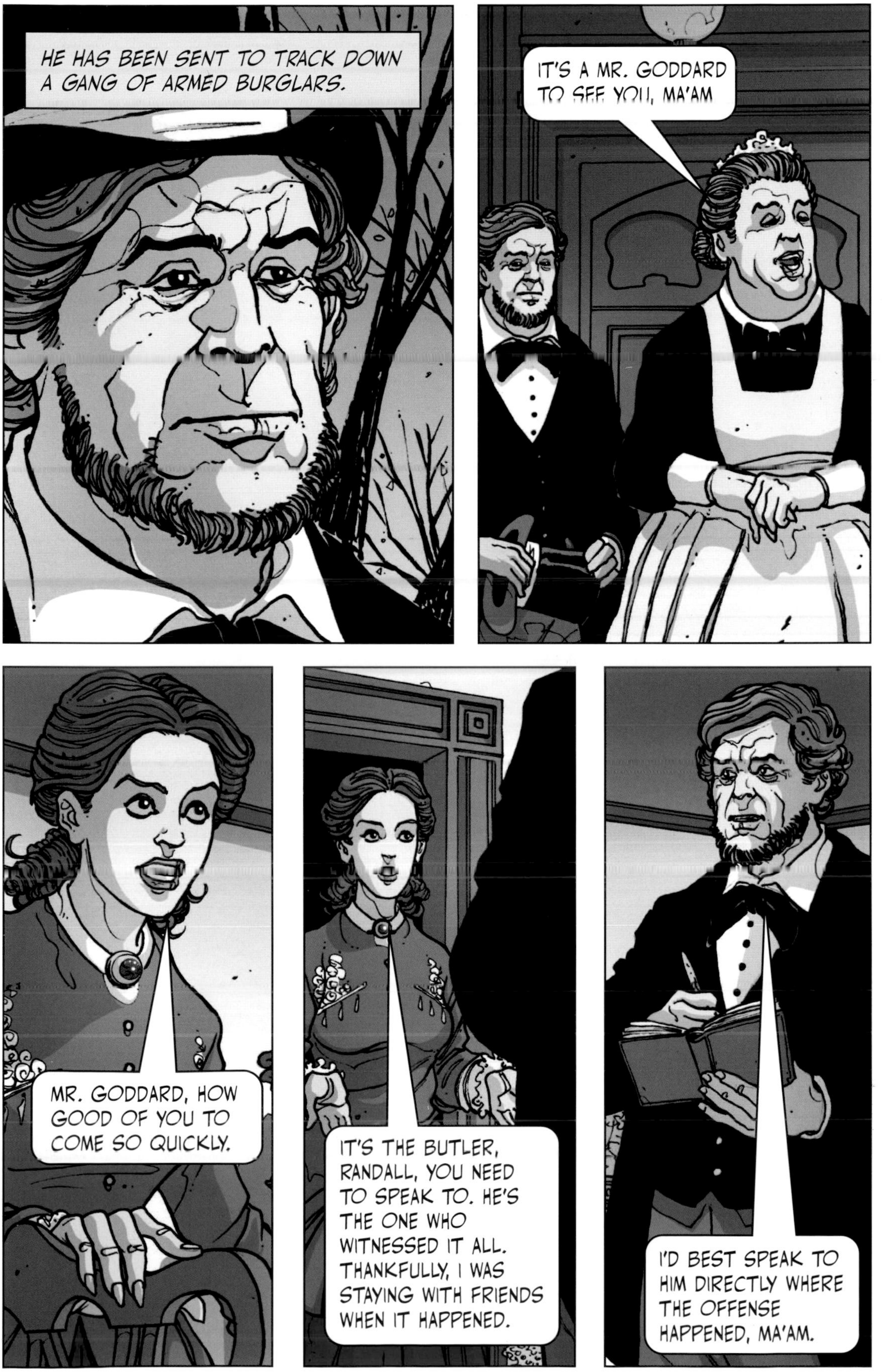
HE HAS BEEN SENT TO TRACK DOWN A GANG OF ARMED BURGLARS.
IT'S A MR. GODDARD TO SEE YOU, MA'AM
MR. GODDARD, HOW GOOD OF YOU TO COME SO QUICKLY.
IT'S THE BUTLER, RANDALL, YOU NEED TO SPEAK TO. HE'S THE ONE WHO WITNESSED IT ALL. THANKFULLY, I WAS STAYING WITH FRIENDS WHEN IT HAPPENED.
I'D BEST SPEAK TO HIM DIRECTLY WHERE THE OFFENSE HAPPENED, MA'AM.

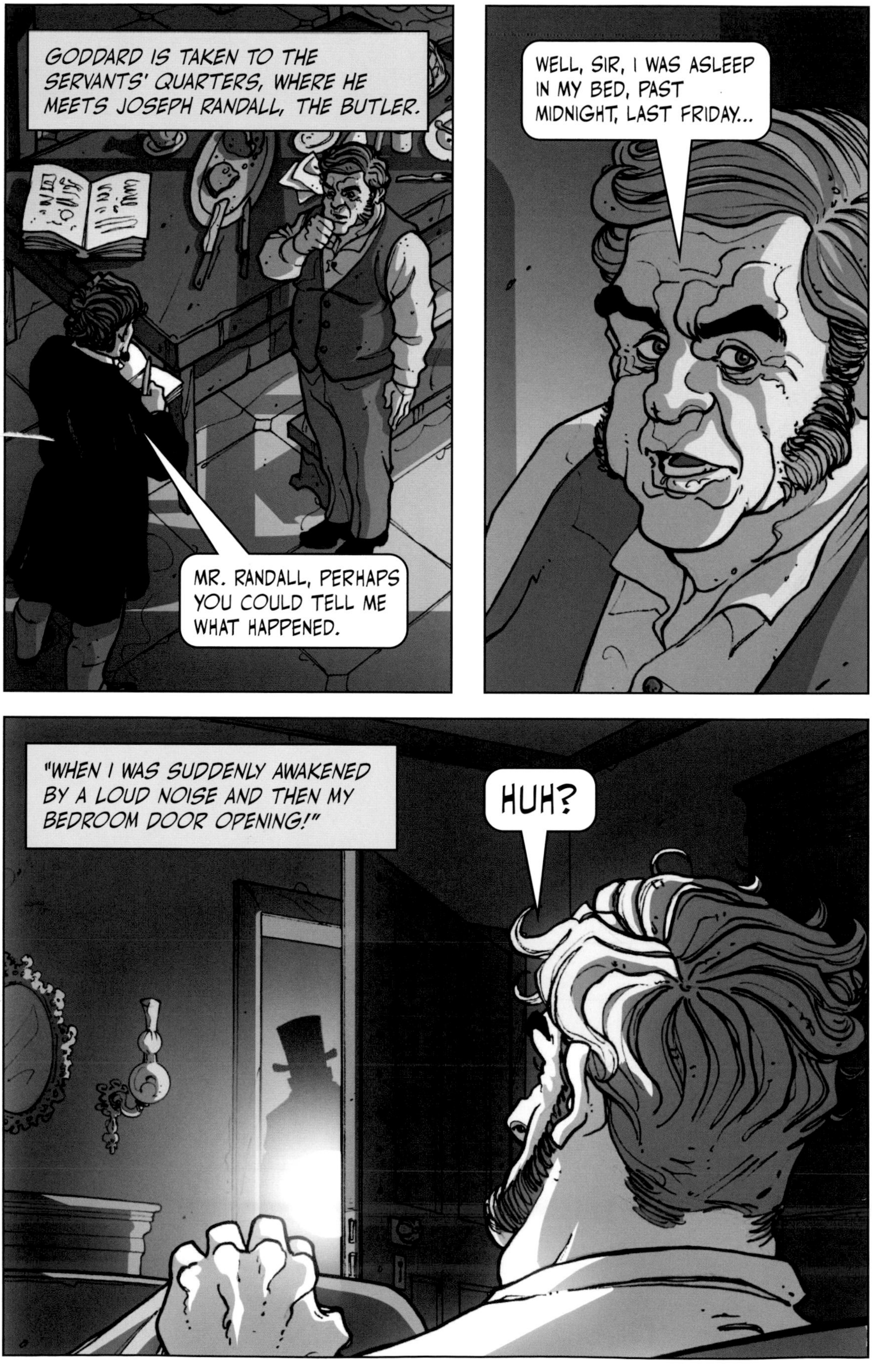
GODDARD IS TAKEN TO THE SERVANTS' QUARTERS, WHERE HE MEETS JOSEPH RANDALL, THE BUTLER.
MR. RANDALL, PERHAPS YOU COULD TELL ME WHAT HAPPENED.
WELL, SIR, I WAS ASLEEP IN MY BED, PAST MIDNIGHT, LAST FRIDAY...
"WHEN I WAS SUDDENLY AWAKENED BY A LOUD NOISE AND THEN MY BEDROOM DOOR OPENING!"
HUH?

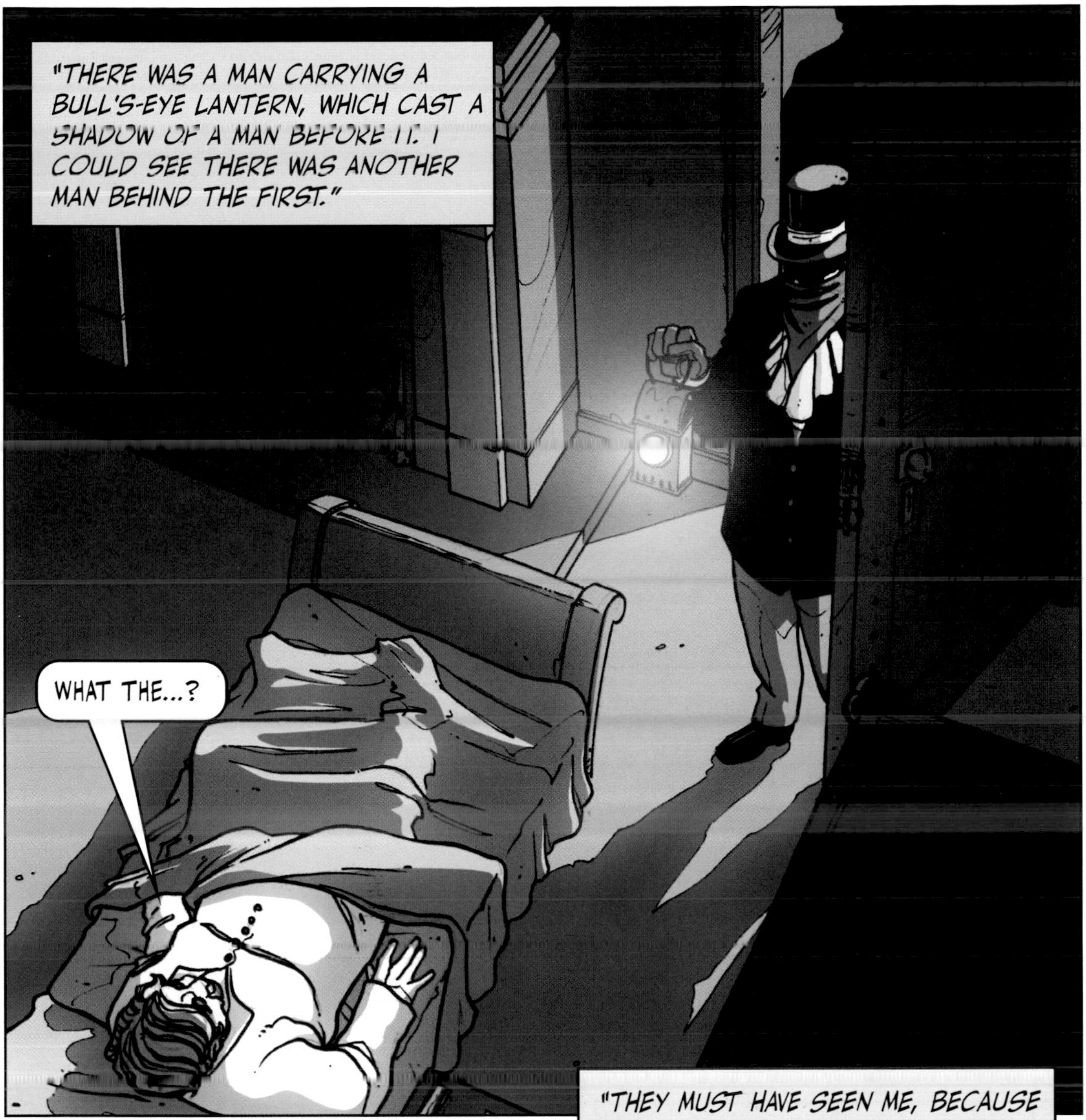
"THERE WAS A MAN CARRYING A BULL'S-EYE LANTERN, WHICH CAST A SHADOW OF A MAN BEFORE IT. I COULD SEE THERE WAS ANOTHER MAN BEHIND THE FIRST."
WHAT THE...?

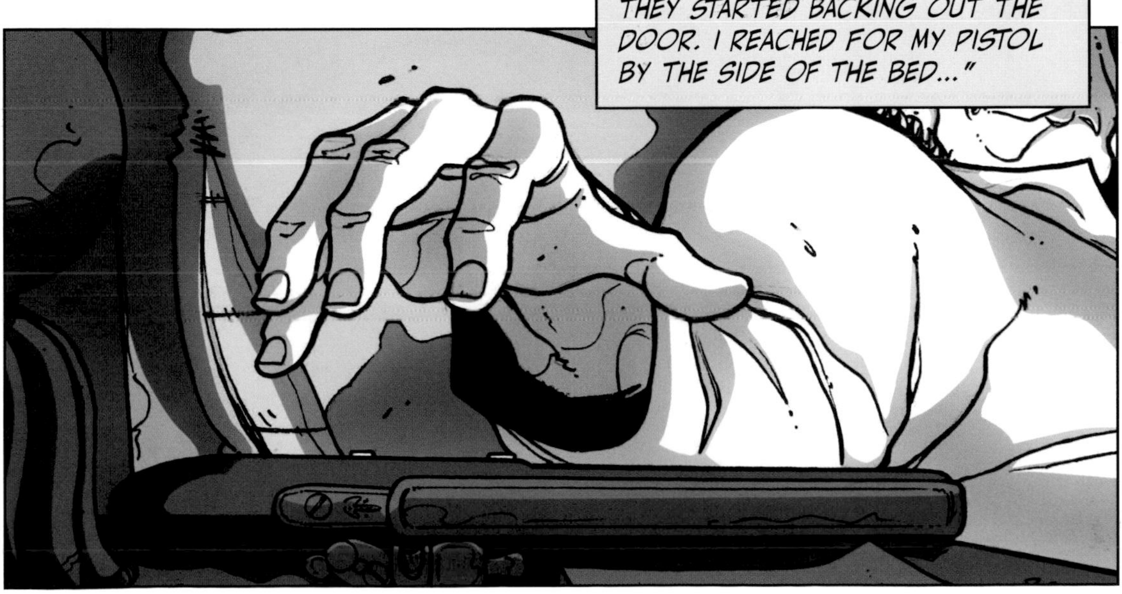
"THEY MUST HAVE SEEN ME, BECAUSE THEY STARTED BACKING OUT THE DOOR. I REACHED FOR MY PISTOL BY THE SIDE OF THE BED..."

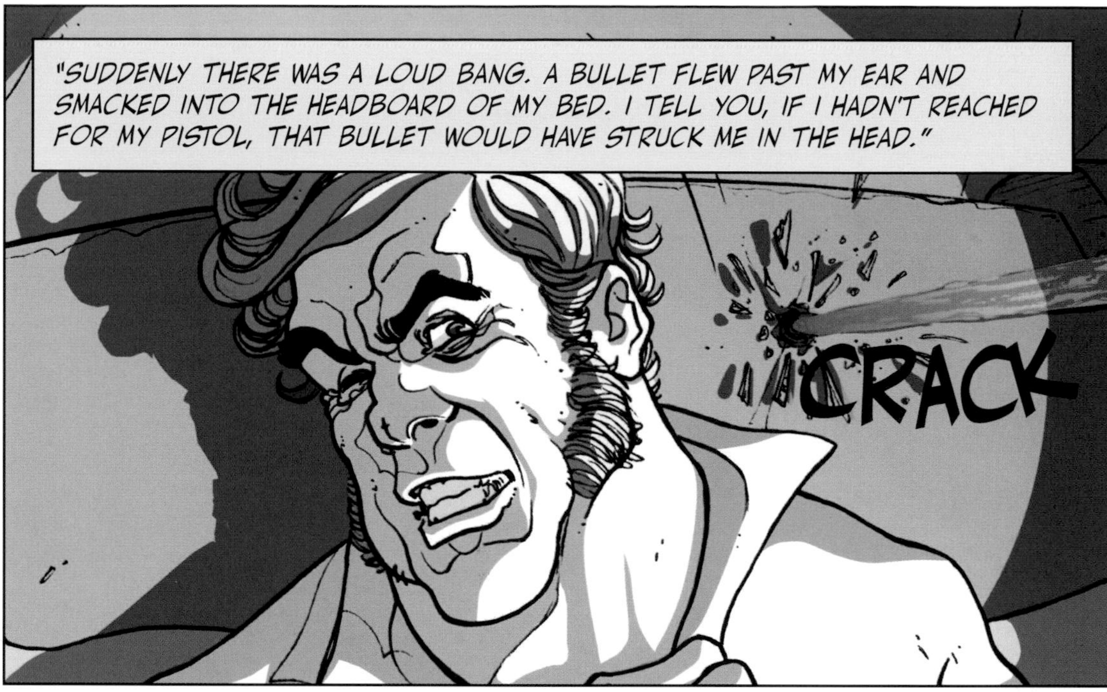
"SUDDENLY THERE WAS A LOUD BANG. A BULLET FLEW PAST MY EAR AND SMACKED INTO THE HEADBOARD OF MY BED. I TELL YOU, IF I HADN'T REACHED FOR MY PISTOL, THAT BULLET WOULD HAVE STRUCK ME IN THE HEAD."
CRACK

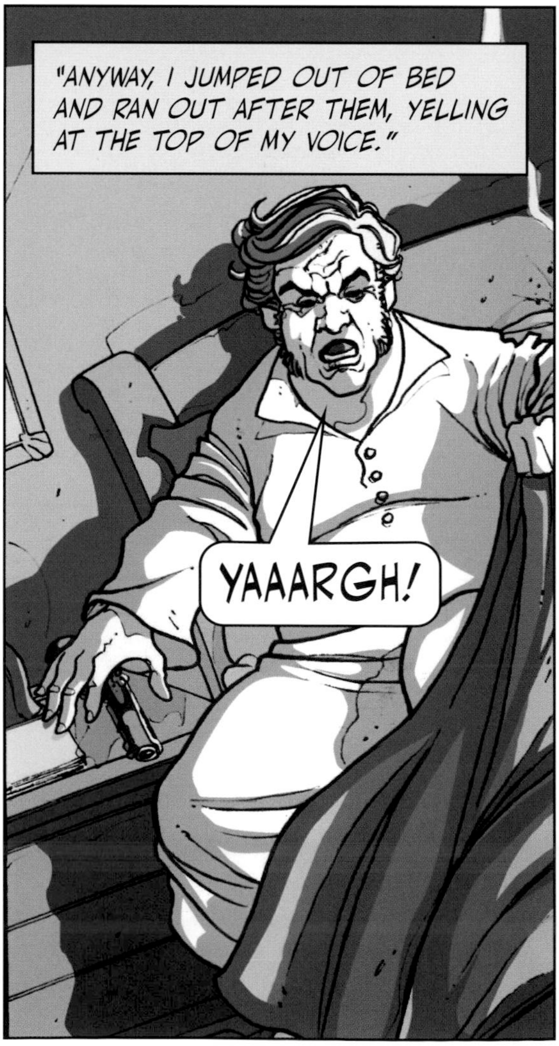
"ANYWAY, I JUMPED OUT OF BED AND RAN OUT AFTER THEM, YELLING AT THE TOP OF MY VOICE."
YAAARGH!

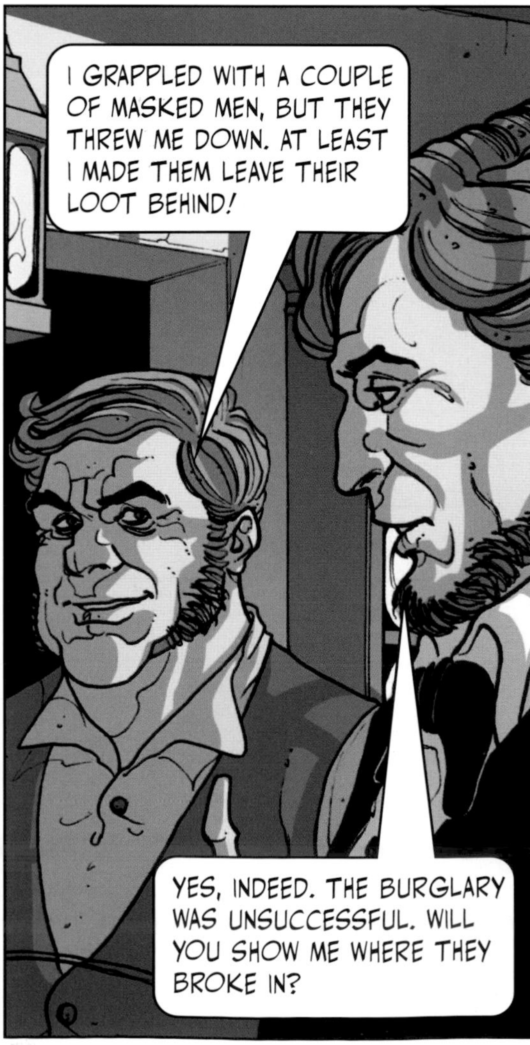
I GRAPPLED WITH A COUPLE OF MASKED MEN, BUT THEY THREW ME DOWN. AT LEAST I MADE THEM LEAVE THEIR LOOT BEHIND!
YES, INDEED. THE BURGLARY WAS UNSUCCESSFUL. WILL YOU SHOW ME WHERE THEY BROKE IN?

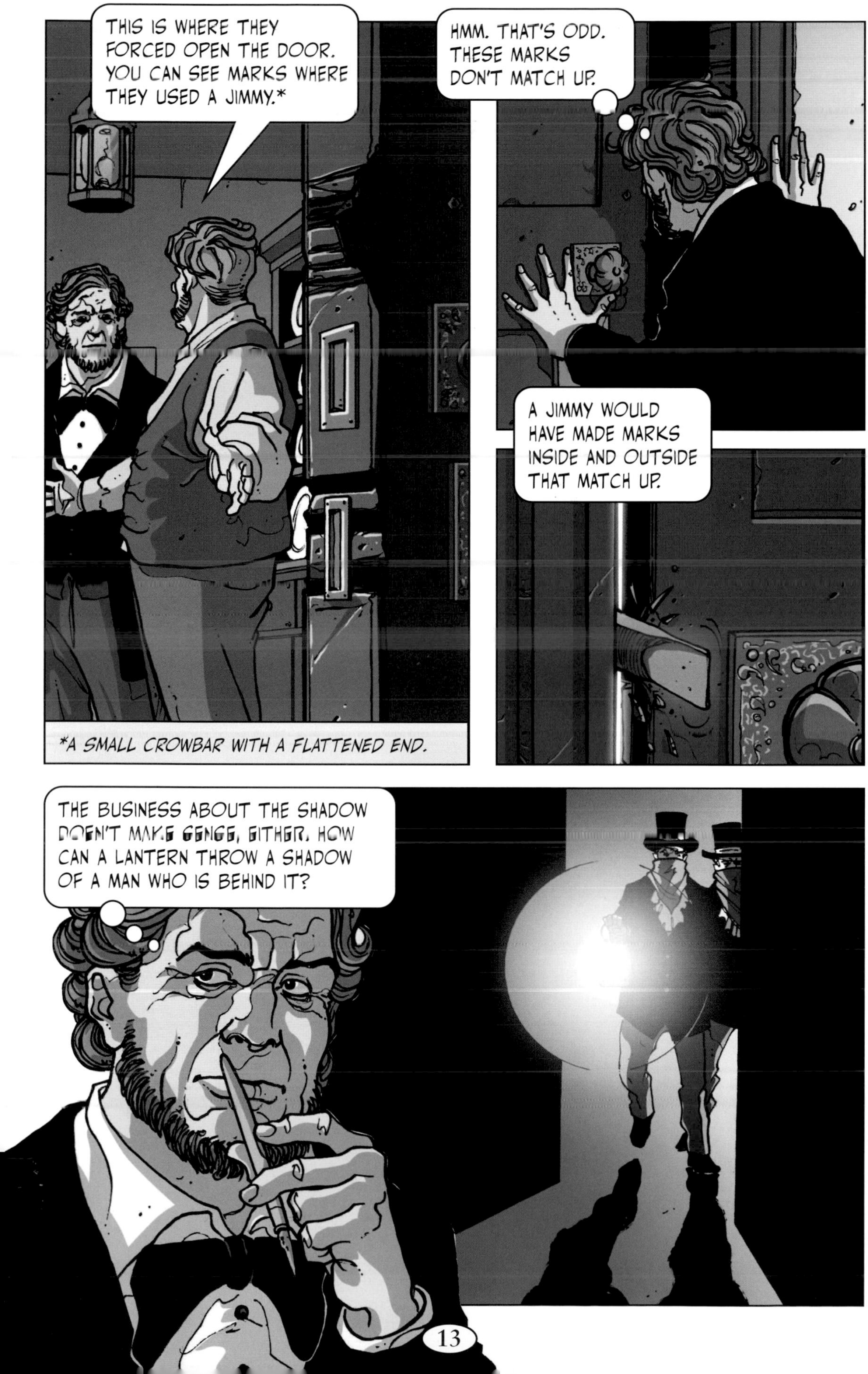
THIS IS WHERE THEY FORCED OPEN THE DOOR. YOU CAN SEE MARKS WHERE THEY USED A JIMMY.*
*A SMALL CROWBAR WITH A FLATTENED END.
HMM. THAT'S ODD. THESE MARKS DON'T MATCH UP.
A JIMMY WOULD HAVE MADE MARKS INSIDE AND OUTSIDE THAT MATCH UP.
THE BUSINESS ABOUT THE SHADOW DOESN'T MAKE SENSE, EITHER. HOW CAN A LANTERN THROW A SHADOW OF A MAN WHO IS BEHIND IT?

THEY MAKE THEIR WAY TO THE BUTLER'S BEDROOM. GODDARD HAS BECOME SUSPICIOUS AND DECIDES TO CHECK OUT THE SHOOTING.

WHERE IS YOUR PISTOL, NOW, MR. RANDALL?

THE BUTLER SHOWS GODDARD HIS PISTOL.

IS THAT YOUR BULLET MOLD?*

YES, IT IS.

*PEOPLE MADE THEIR OWN BULLETS BY POURING MOLTEN LEAD INTO A MOLD.

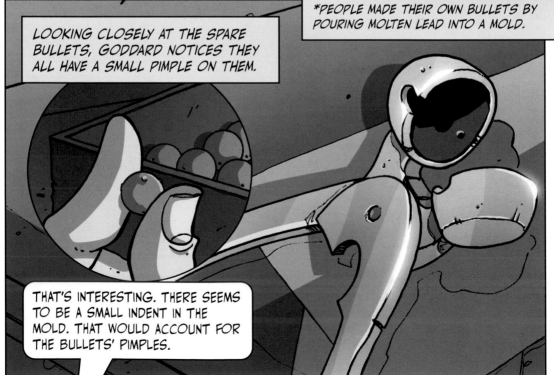

LOOKING CLOSELY AT THE SPARE BULLETS, GODDARD NOTICES THEY ALL HAVE A SMALL PIMPLE ON THEM.

THAT'S INTERESTING. THERE SEEMS TO BE A SMALL INDENT IN THE MOLD. THAT WOULD ACCOUNT FOR THE BULLETS' PIMPLES.

GODDARD HAS AN IDEA.

CAN YOU GIVE ME THE BULLET THAT STRUCK THE HEADBOARD?

HERE IT IS. I DUG IT OUT THE NEXT DAY AND KEPT IT SAFE.

THE BULLET IS SLIGHTLY FLATTENED BY ITS IMPACT WITH THE HEADBOARD.

JUST AS I THOUGHT. THIS ONE ALSO HAS A PIMPLE ON IT.

GODDARD LEAVES THE HOUSE, PROMISING TO RETURN THE NEXT DAY. HE TAKES THE PISTOL, BULLETS, AND MOLD WITH HIM.

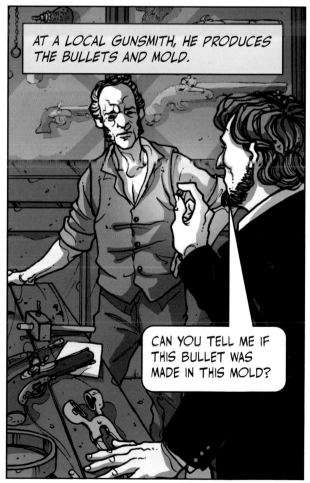

AT A LOCAL GUNSMITH, HE PRODUCES THE BULLETS AND MOLD.

CAN YOU TELL ME IF THIS BULLET WAS MADE IN THIS MOLD?

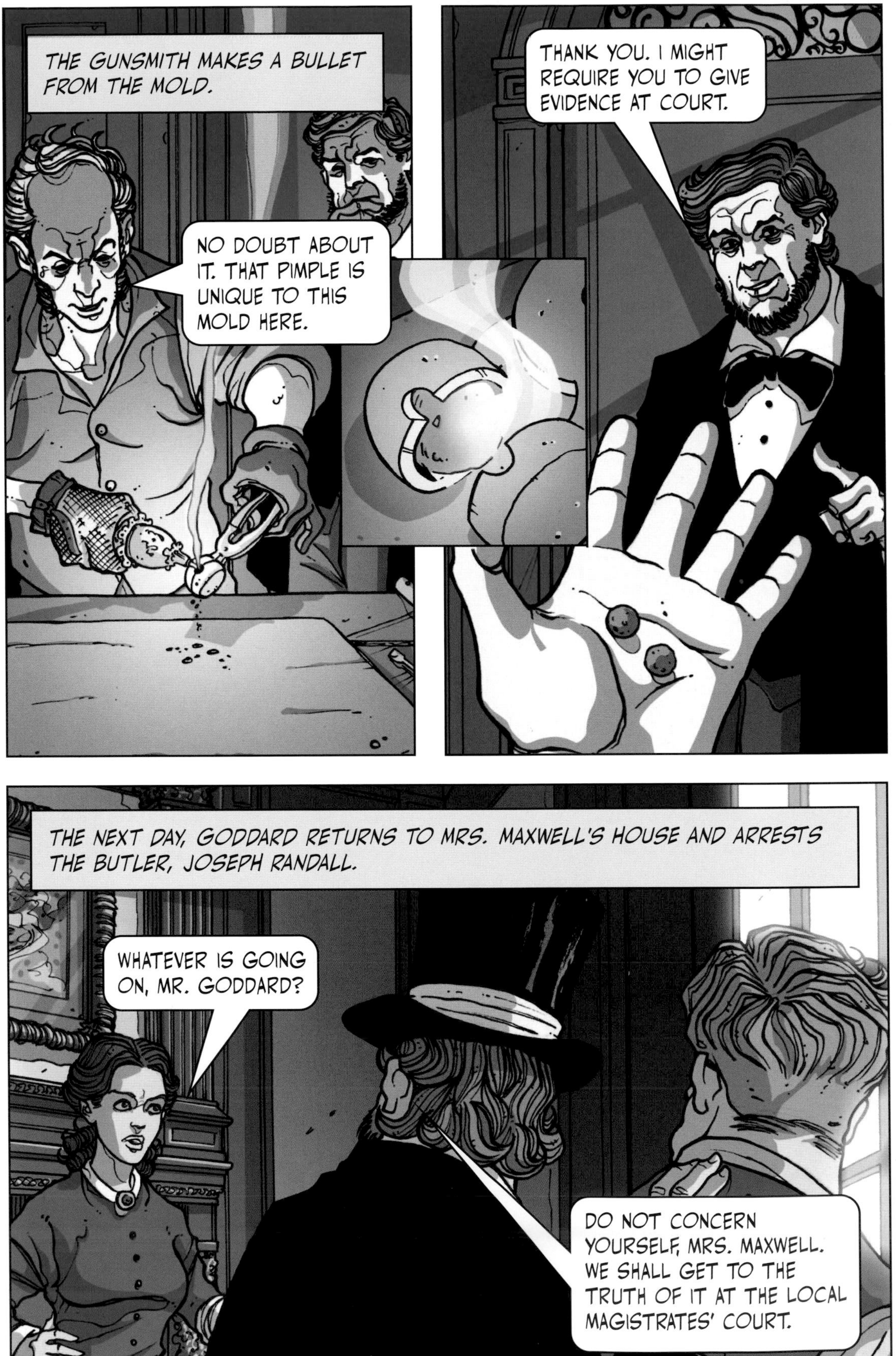
THE GUNSMITH MAKES A BULLET FROM THE MOLD.
NO DOUBT ABOUT IT. THAT PIMPLE IS UNIQUE TO THIS MOLD HERE.
THANK YOU. I MIGHT REQUIRE YOU TO GIVE EVIDENCE AT COURT.
THE NEXT DAY, GODDARD RETURNS TO MRS. MAXWELL'S HOUSE AND ARRESTS THE BUTLER, JOSEPH RANDALL.
WHATEVER IS GOING ON, MR. GODDARD?
DO NOT CONCERN YOURSELF, MRS. MAXWELL. WE SHALL GET TO THE TRUTH OF IT AT THE LOCAL MAGISTRATES' COURT.

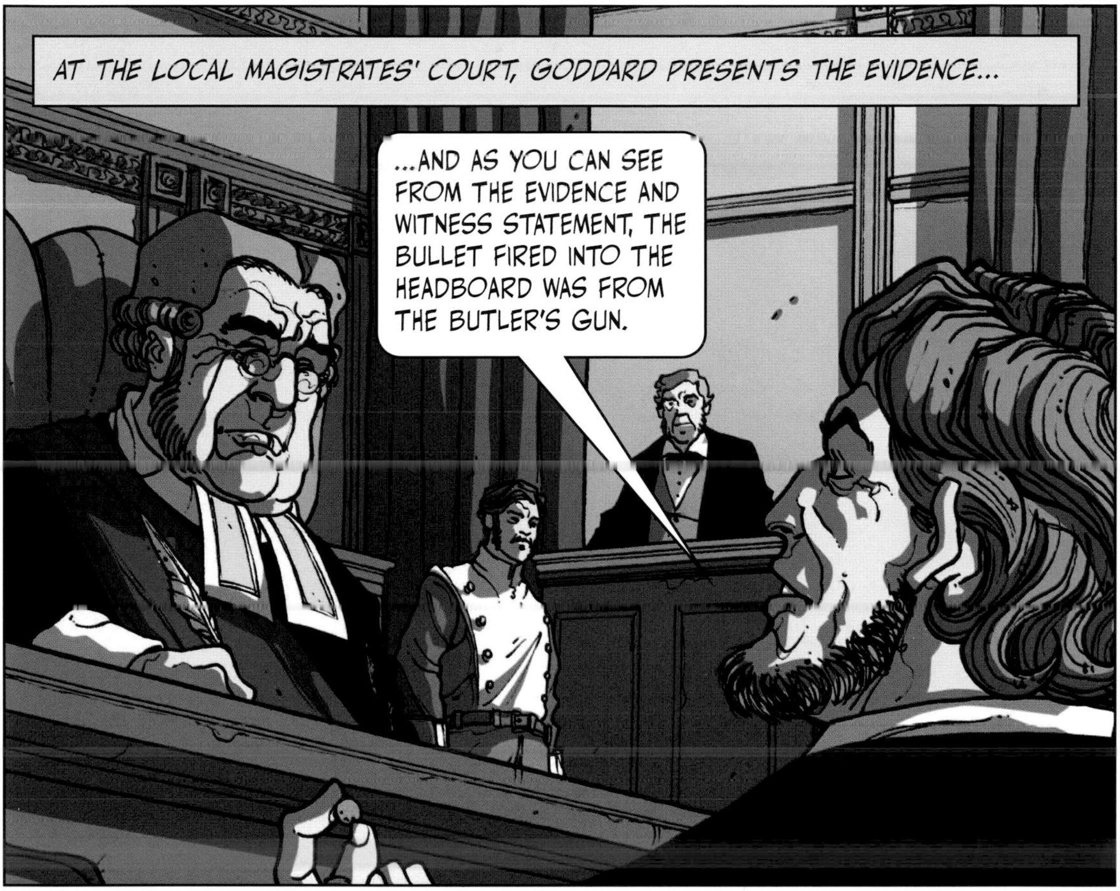
AT THE LOCAL MAGISTRATES' COURT, GODDARD PRESENTS THE EVIDENCE...
...AND AS YOU CAN SEE FROM THE EVIDENCE AND WITNESS STATEMENT, THE BULLET FIRED INTO THE HEADBOARD WAS FROM THE BUTLER'S GUN.

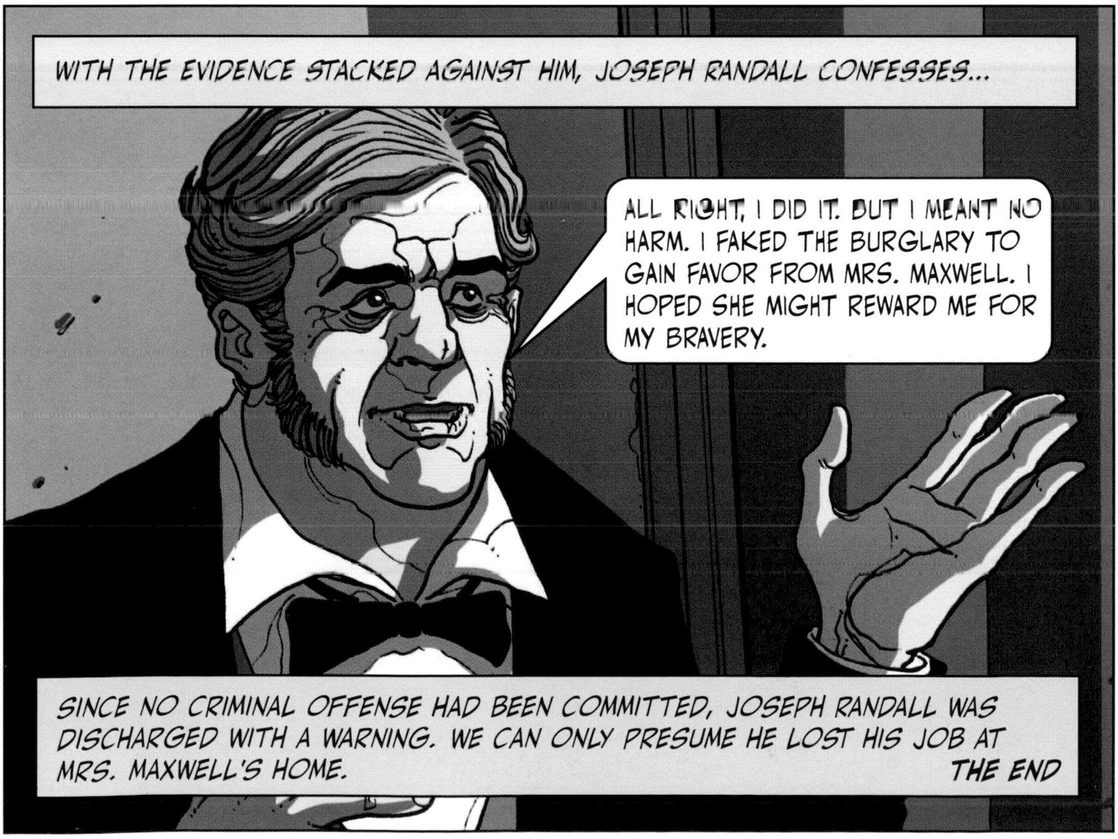
WITH THE EVIDENCE STACKED AGAINST HIM, JOSEPH RANDALL CONFESSES...
ALL RIGHT, I DID IT. BUT I MEANT NO HARM. I FAKED THE BURGLARY TO GAIN FAVOR FROM MRS. MAXWELL. I HOPED SHE MIGHT REWARD ME FOR MY BRAVERY.
SINCE NO CRIMINAL OFFENSE HAD BEEN COMMITTED, JOSEPH RANDALL WAS DISCHARGED WITH A WARNING. WE CAN ONLY PRESUME HE LOST HIS JOB AT MRS. MAXWELL'S HOME.
THE END

THE BULLET IN THE TREE

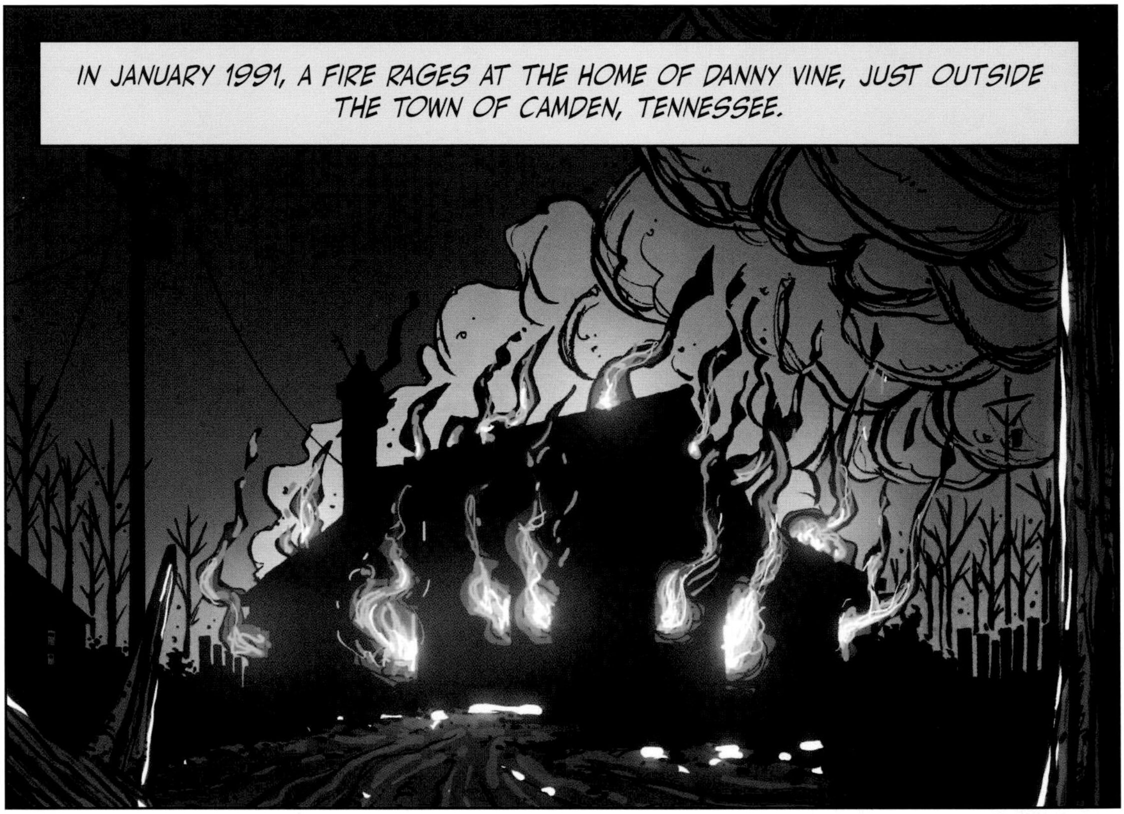
IN JANUARY 1991, A FIRE RAGES AT THE HOME OF DANNY VINE, JUST OUTSIDE THE TOWN OF CAMDEN, TENNESSEE.

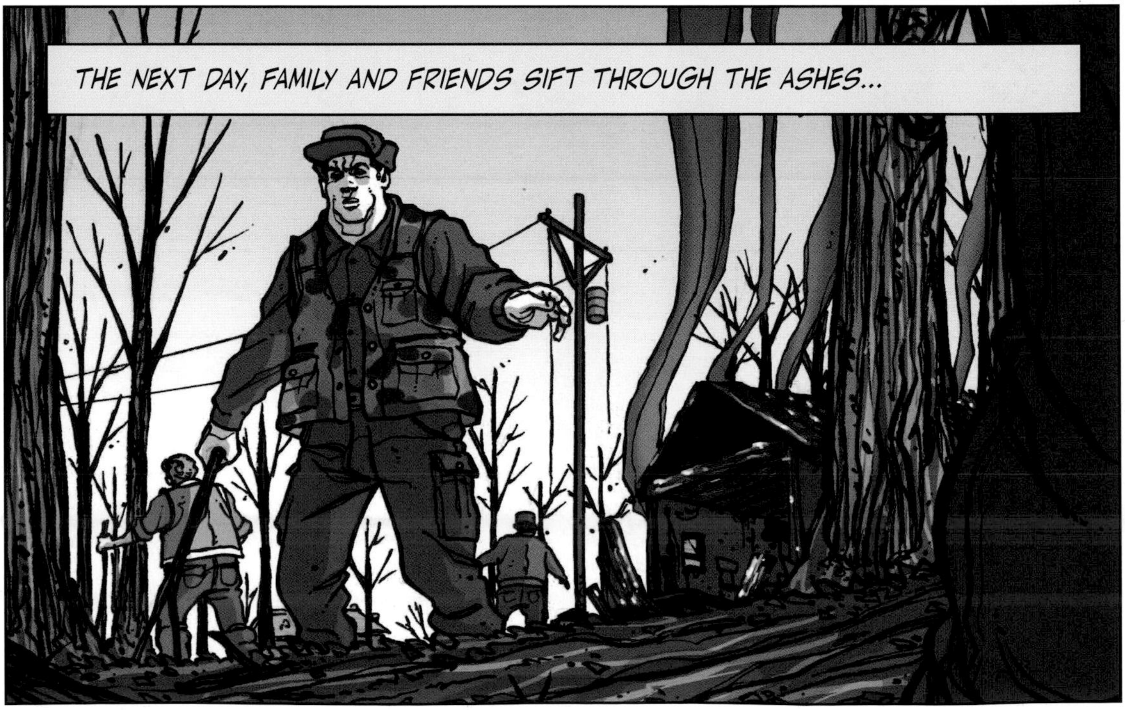
THE NEXT DAY, FAMILY AND FRIENDS SIFT THROUGH THE ASHES...

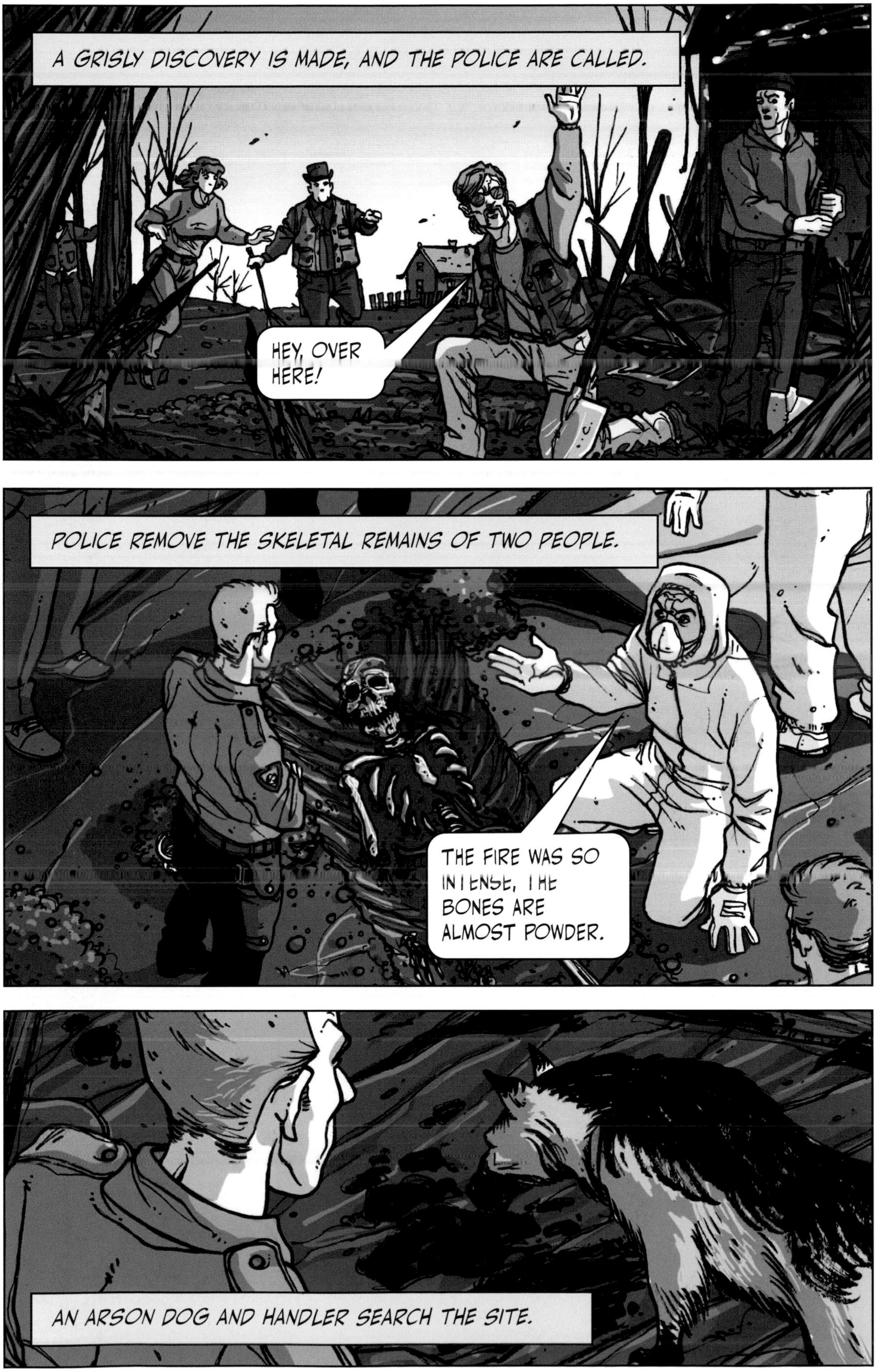
A GRISLY DISCOVERY IS MADE, AND THE POLICE ARE CALLED.
HEY, OVER HERE!
POLICE REMOVE THE SKELETAL REMAINS OF TWO PEOPLE.
THE FIRE WAS SO INTENSE, THE BONES ARE ALMOST POWDER.
AN ARSON DOG AND HANDLER SEARCH THE SITE.

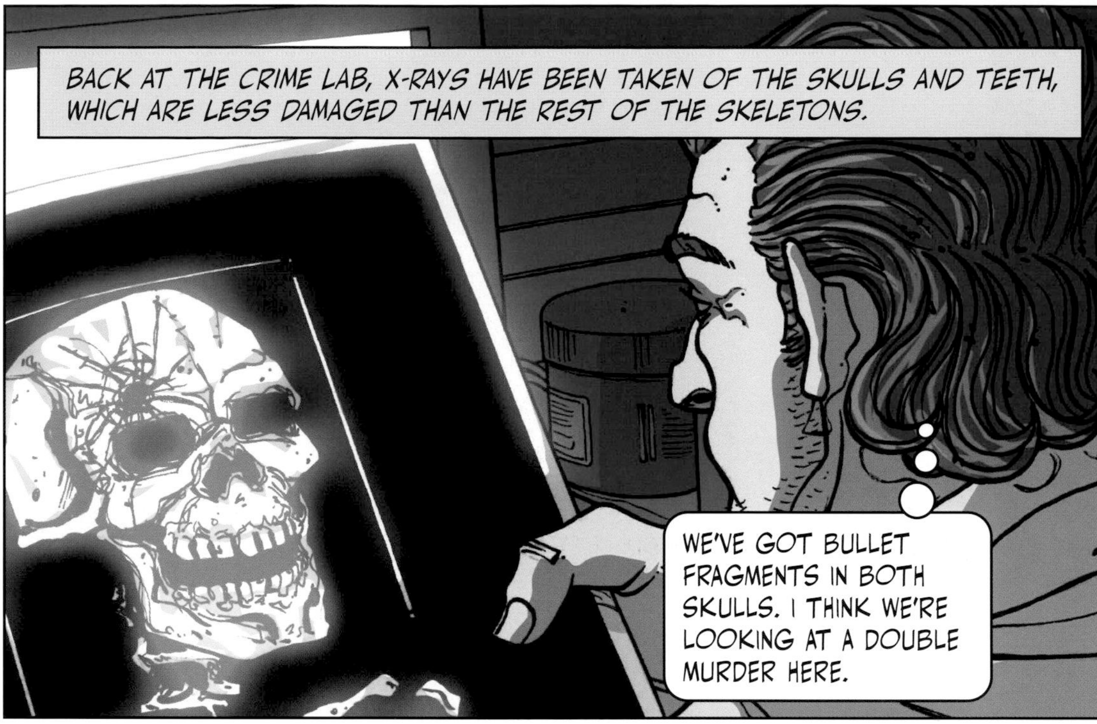
BACK AT THE CRIME LAB, X-RAYS HAVE BEEN TAKEN OF THE SKULLS AND TEETH, WHICH ARE LESS DAMAGED THAN THE REST OF THE SKELETONS.
WE'VE GOT BULLET FRAGMENTS IN BOTH SKULLS. I THINK WE'RE LOOKING AT A DOUBLE MURDER HERE.

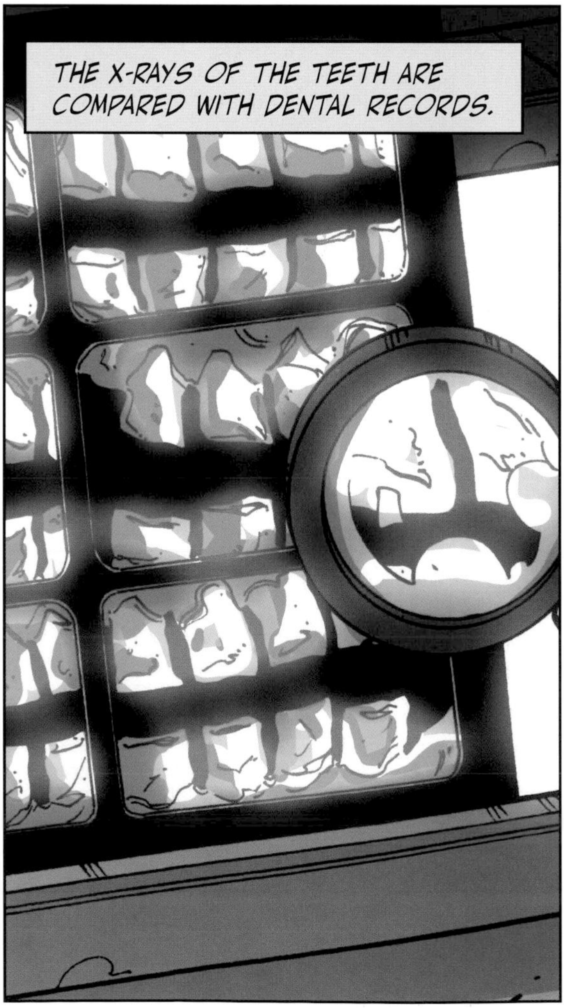
THE X-RAYS OF THE TEETH ARE COMPARED WITH DENTAL RECORDS.

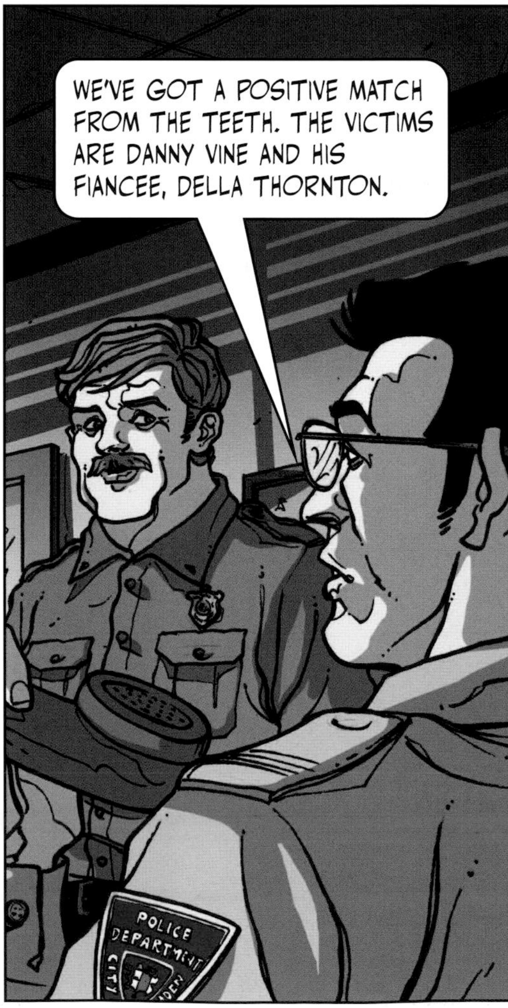
WE'VE GOT A POSITIVE MATCH FROM THE TEETH. THE VICTIMS ARE DANNY VINE AND HIS FIANCEE, DELLA THORNTON.
POLICE DEPARTMENT

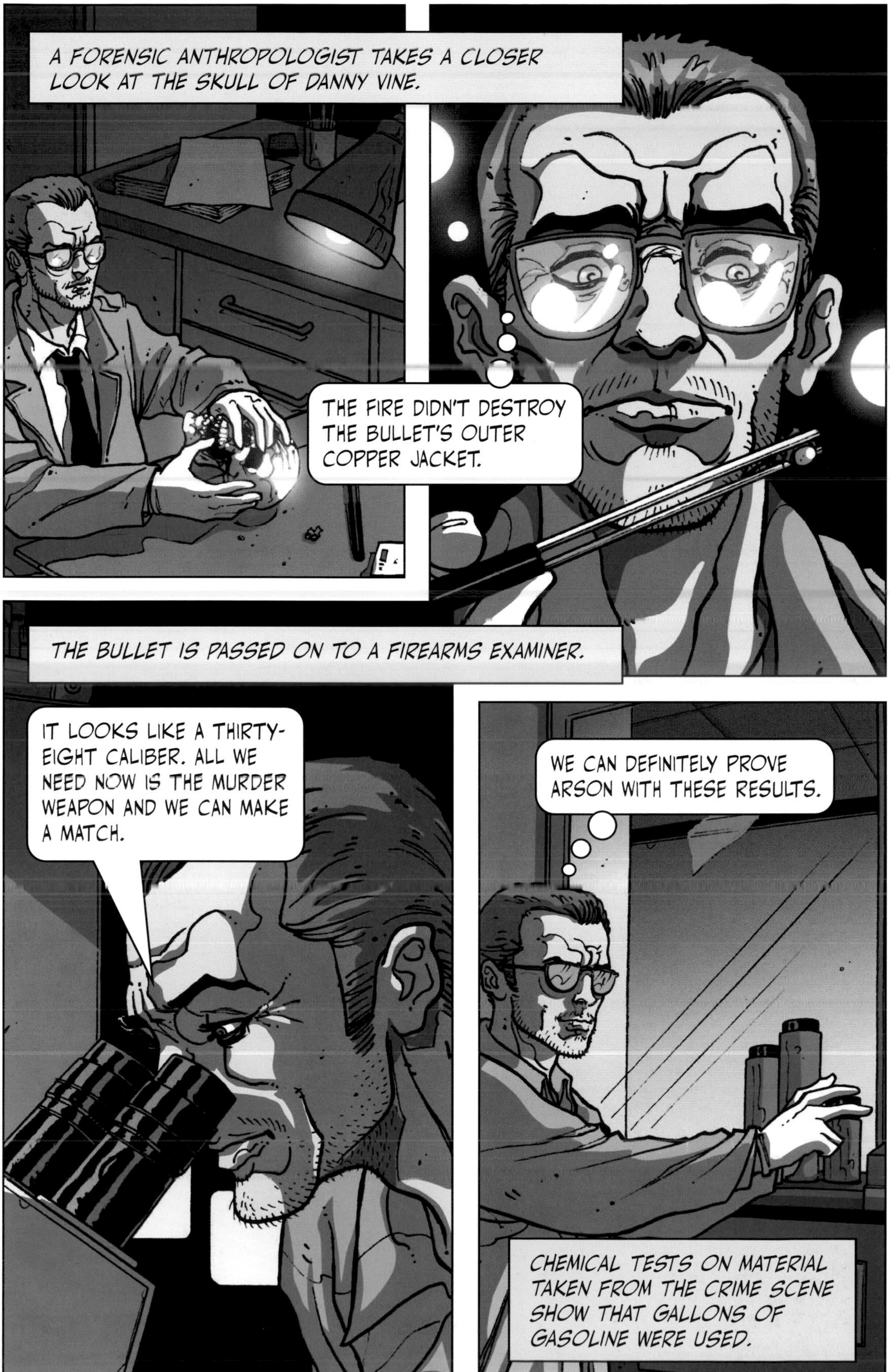
A FORENSIC ANTHROPOLOGIST TAKES A CLOSER LOOK AT THE SKULL OF DANNY VINE.
THE FIRE DIDN'T DESTROY THE BULLET'S OUTER COPPER JACKET.
THE BULLET IS PASSED ON TO A FIREARMS EXAMINER.
IT LOOKS LIKE A THIRTY-EIGHT CALIBER. ALL WE NEED NOW IS THE MURDER WEAPON AND WE CAN MAKE A MATCH.
WE CAN DEFINITELY PROVE ARSON WITH THESE RESULTS.
CHEMICAL TESTS ON MATERIAL TAKEN FROM THE CRIME SCENE SHOW THAT GALLONS OF GASOLINE WERE USED.

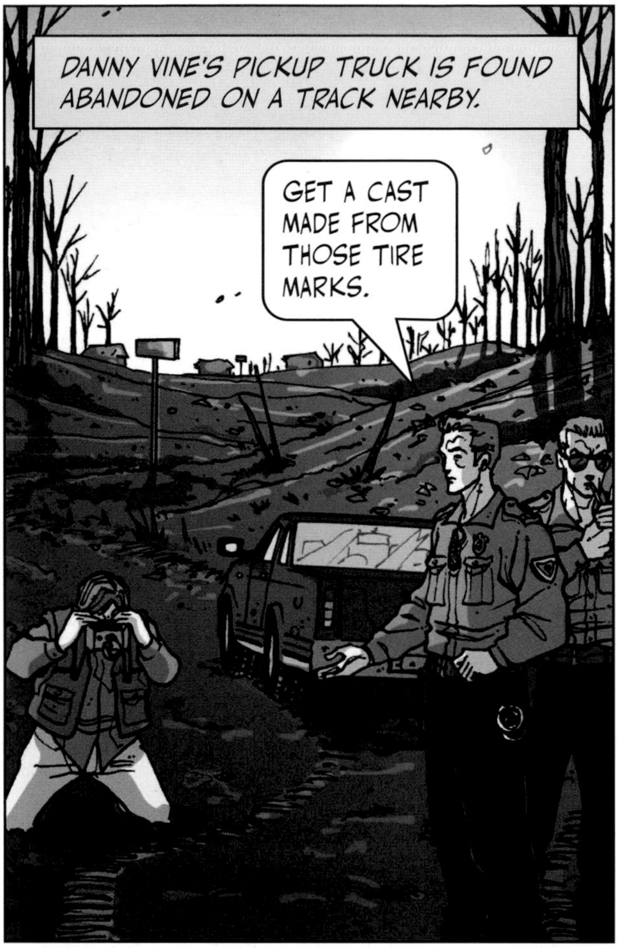
DANNY VINE'S PICKUP TRUCK IS FOUND ABANDONED ON A TRACK NEARBY.
GET A CAST MADE FROM THOSE TIRE MARKS.

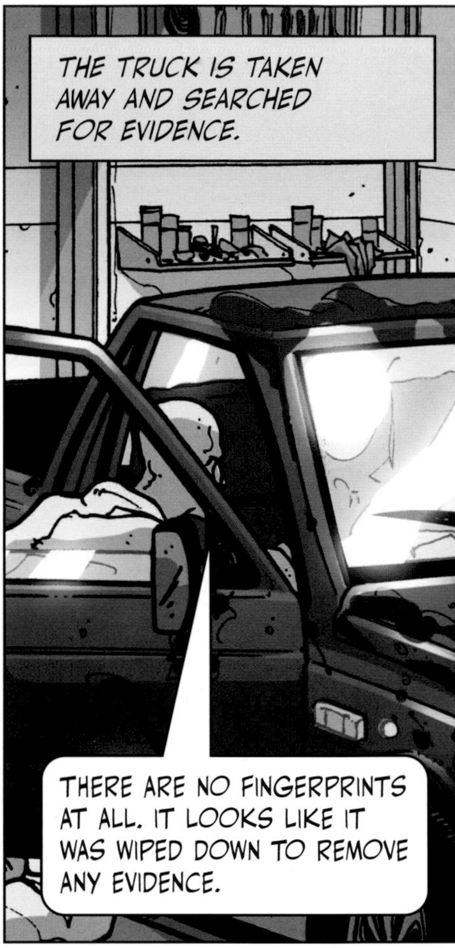
THE TRUCK IS TAKEN AWAY AND SEARCHED FOR EVIDENCE.
THERE ARE NO FINGERPRINTS AT ALL. IT LOOKS LIKE IT WAS WIPED DOWN TO REMOVE ANY EVIDENCE.

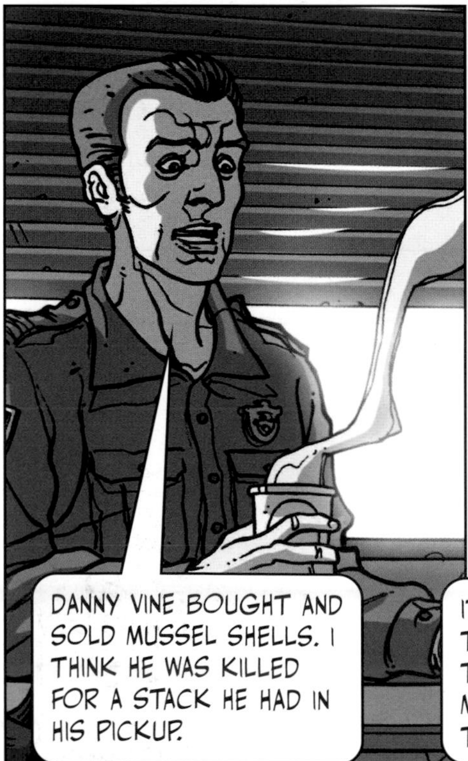
DANNY VINE BOUGHT AND SOLD MUSSEL SHELLS. I THINK HE WAS KILLED FOR A STACK HE HAD IN HIS PICKUP.

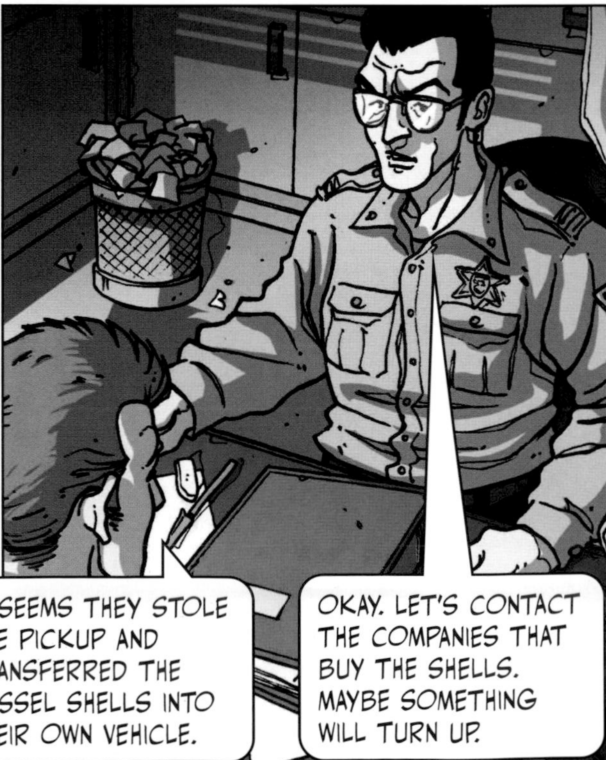
IT SEEMS THEY STOLE THE PICKUP AND TRANSFERRED THE MUSSEL SHELLS INTO THEIR OWN VEHICLE.
OKAY. LET'S CONTACT THE COMPANIES THAT BUY THE SHELLS. MAYBE SOMETHING WILL TURN UP.

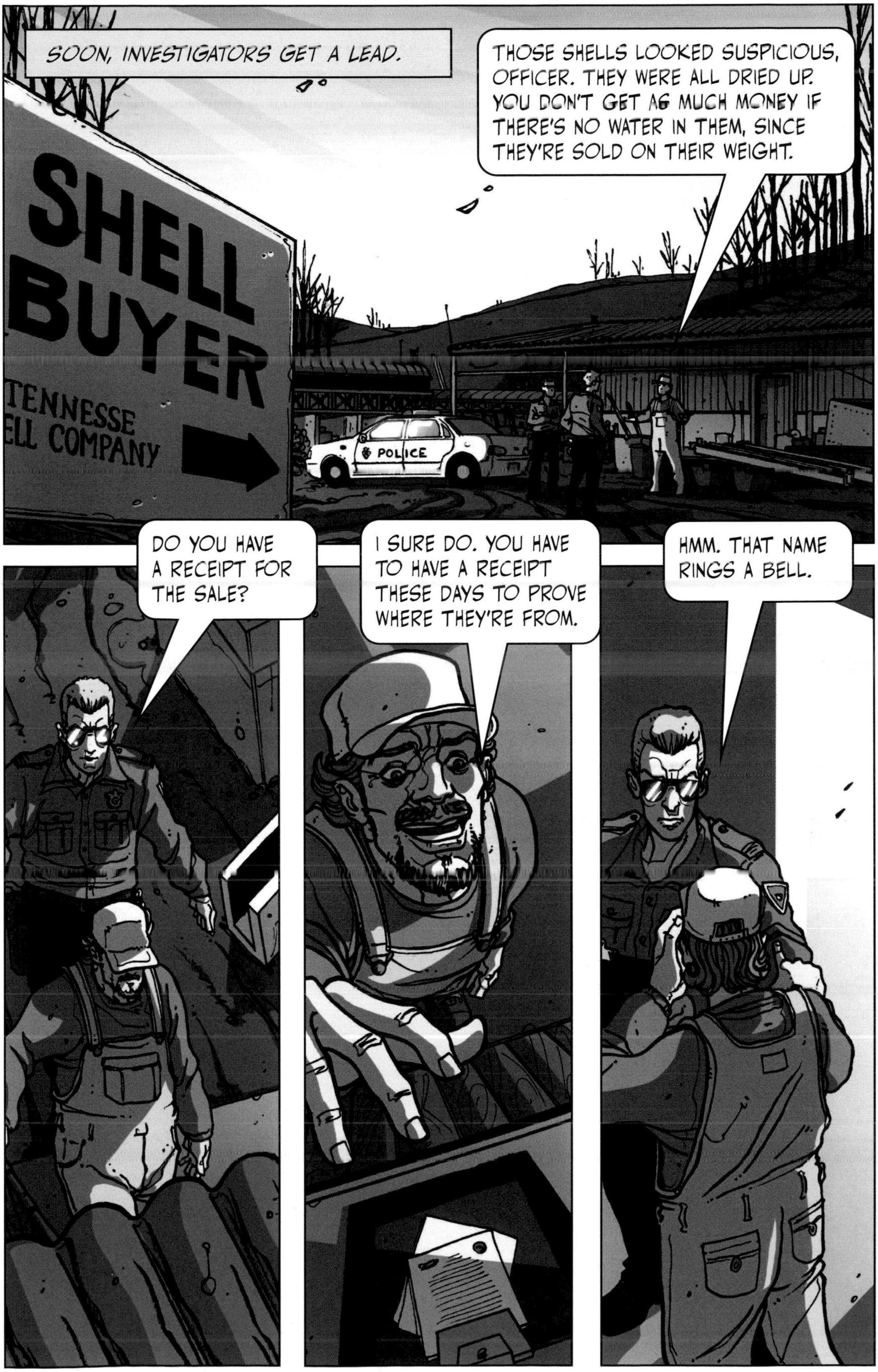
SOON, INVESTIGATORS GET A LEAD.
THOSE SHELLS LOOKED SUSPICIOUS, OFFICER. THEY WERE ALL DRIED UP. YOU DON'T GET AS MUCH MONEY IF THERE'S NO WATER IN THEM, SINCE THEY'RE SOLD ON THEIR WEIGHT.
SHELL BUYER
TENNESSE
ELL COMPANY
POLICE
DO YOU HAVE A RECEIPT FOR THE SALE?
I SURE DO. YOU HAVE TO HAVE A RECEIPT THESE DAYS TO PROVE WHERE THEY'RE FROM.
HMM. THAT NAME RINGS A BELL.

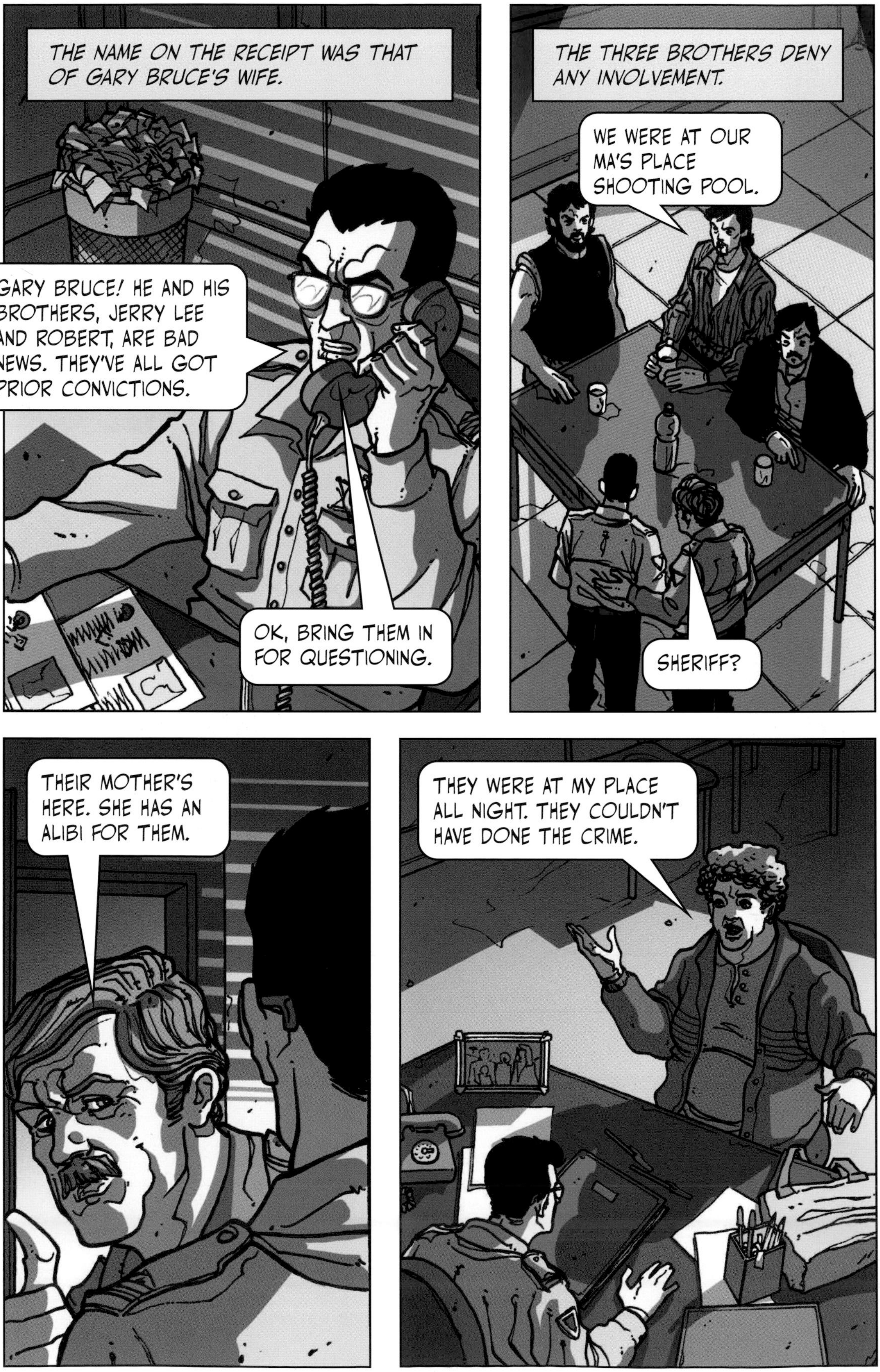
THE NAME ON THE RECEIPT WAS THAT OF GARY BRUCE'S WIFE.
GARY BRUCE! HE AND HIS BROTHERS, JERRY LEE AND ROBERT, ARE BAD NEWS. THEY'VE ALL GOT PRIOR CONVICTIONS.
OK, BRING THEM IN FOR QUESTIONING.
THE THREE BROTHERS DENY ANY INVOLVEMENT.
WE WERE AT OUR MA'S PLACE SHOOTING POOL.
SHERIFF?
THEIR MOTHER'S HERE. SHE HAS AN ALIBI FOR THEM.
THEY WERE AT MY PLACE ALL NIGHT. THEY COULDN'T HAVE DONE THE CRIME.

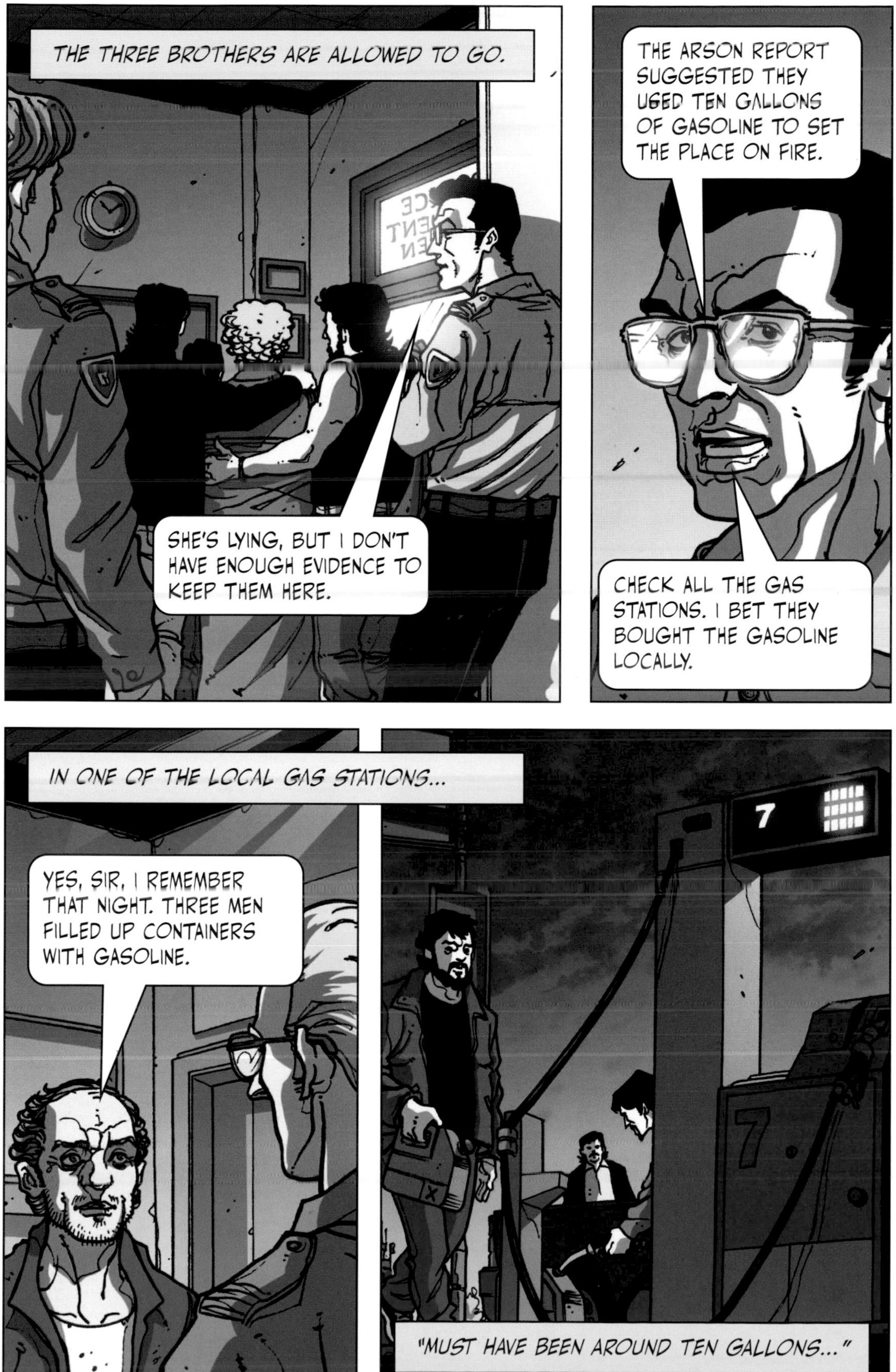
THE THREE BROTHERS ARE ALLOWED TO GO.
SHE'S LYING, BUT I DON'T HAVE ENOUGH EVIDENCE TO KEEP THEM HERE.
THE ARSON REPORT SUGGESTED THEY USED TEN GALLONS OF GASOLINE TO SET THE PLACE ON FIRE.
CHECK ALL THE GAS STATIONS. I BET THEY BOUGHT THE GASOLINE LOCALLY.
IN ONE OF THE LOCAL GAS STATIONS...
YES, SIR, I REMEMBER THAT NIGHT. THREE MEN FILLED UP CONTAINERS WITH GASOLINE.
7
"MUST HAVE BEEN AROUND TEN GALLONS..."

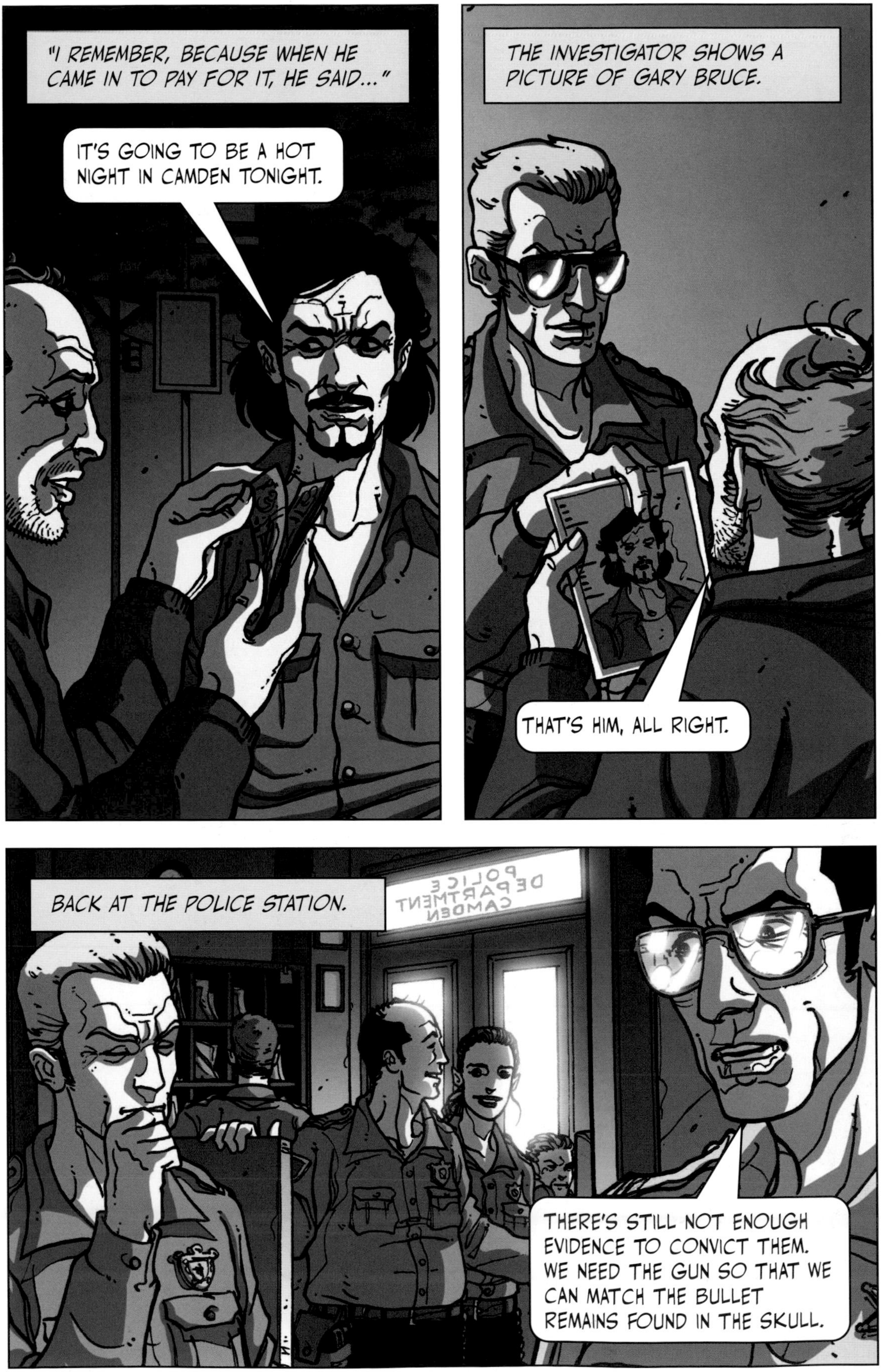
"I REMEMBER, BECAUSE WHEN HE CAME IN TO PAY FOR IT, HE SAID..."
IT'S GOING TO BE A HOT NIGHT IN CAMDEN TONIGHT.
THE INVESTIGATOR SHOWS A PICTURE OF GARY BRUCE.
THAT'S HIM, ALL RIGHT.
BACK AT THE POLICE STATION.
THERE'S STILL NOT ENOUGH EVIDENCE TO CONVICT THEM. WE NEED THE GUN SO THAT WE CAN MATCH THE BULLET REMAINS FOUND IN THE SKULL.

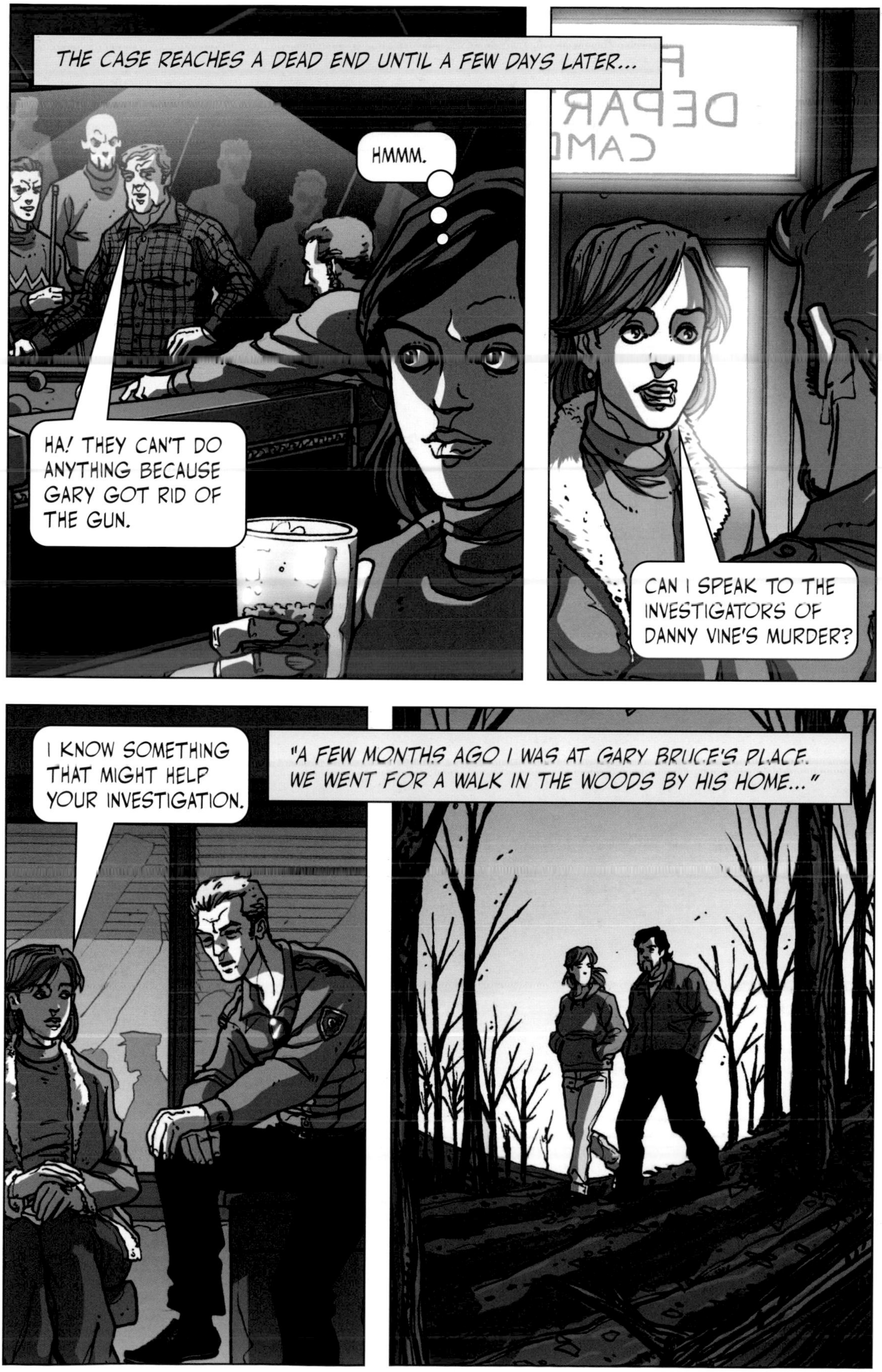
THE CASE REACHES A DEAD END UNTIL A FEW DAYS LATER...
HMMM.
HA! THEY CAN'T DO ANYTHING BECAUSE GARY GOT RID OF THE GUN.
CAN I SPEAK TO THE INVESTIGATORS OF DANNY VINE'S MURDER?
I KNOW SOMETHING THAT MIGHT HELP YOUR INVESTIGATION.
"A FEW MONTHS AGO I WAS AT GARY BRUCE'S PLACE. WE WENT FOR A WALK IN THE WOODS BY HIS HOME..."

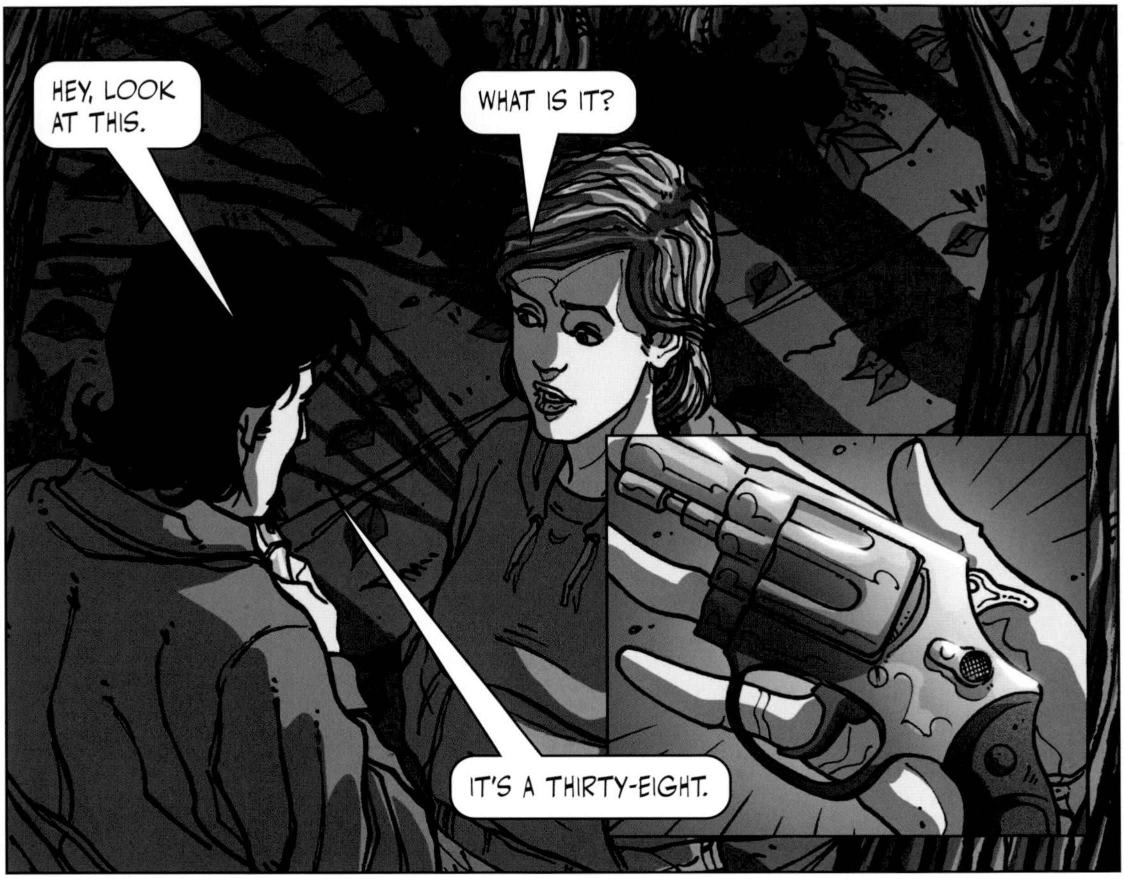
HEY, LOOK AT THIS.
WHAT IS IT?
IT'S A THIRTY-EIGHT.

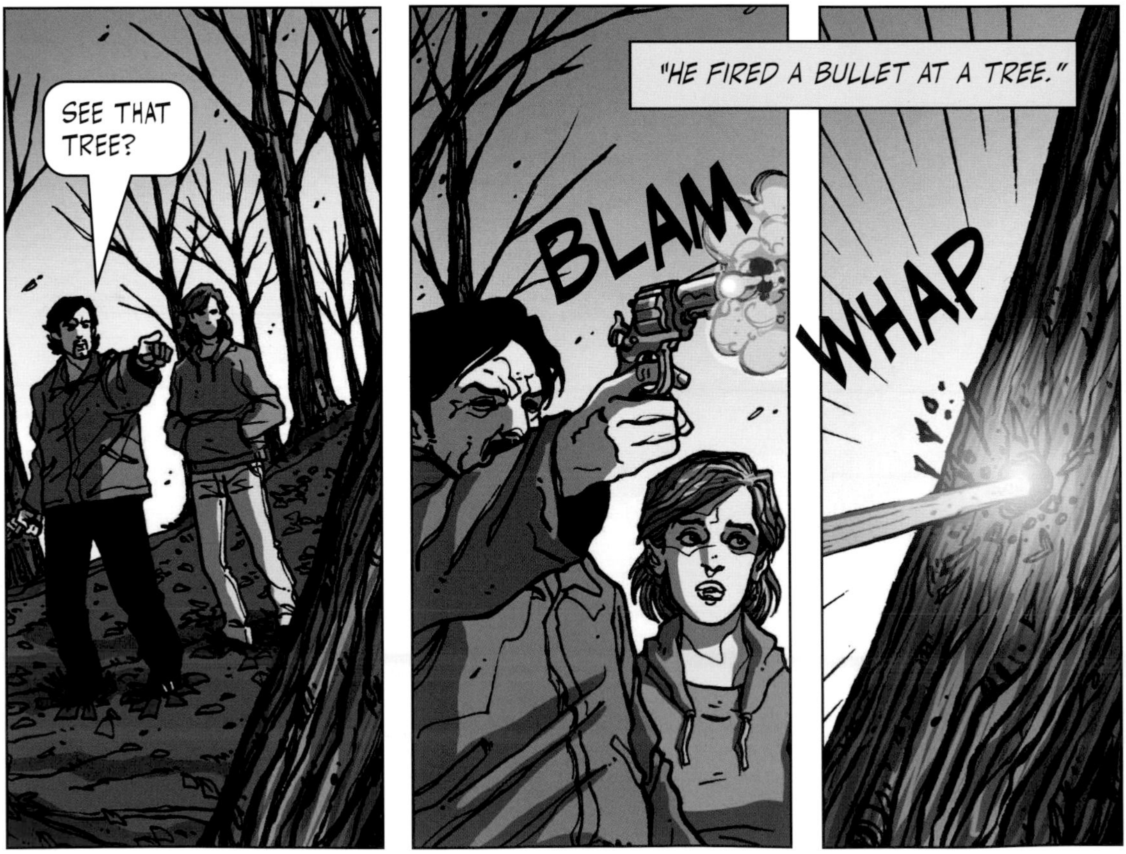
SEE THAT TREE?
"HE FIRED A BULLET AT A TREE."
BLAM
WHAP

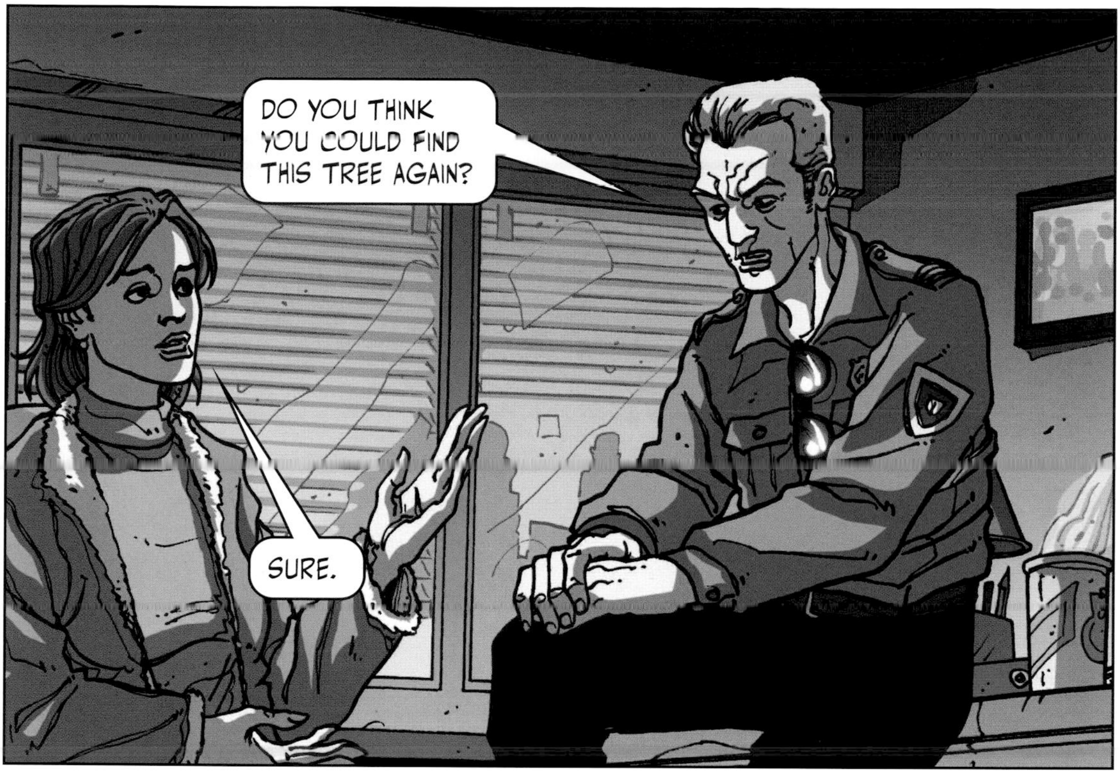
DO YOU THINK YOU COULD FIND THIS TREE AGAIN?
SURE.

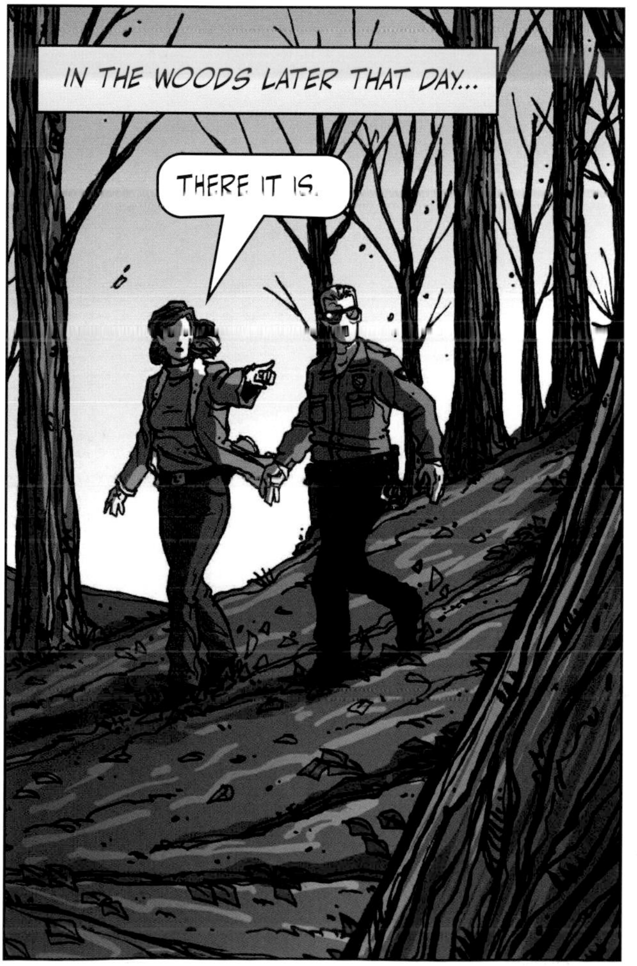
IN THE WOODS LATER THAT DAY...
THERE IT IS.

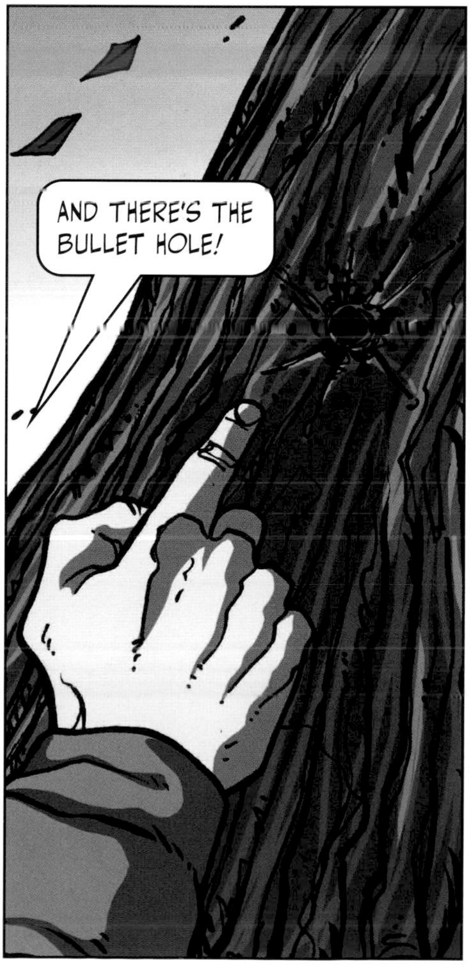
AND THERE'S THE BULLET HOLE!

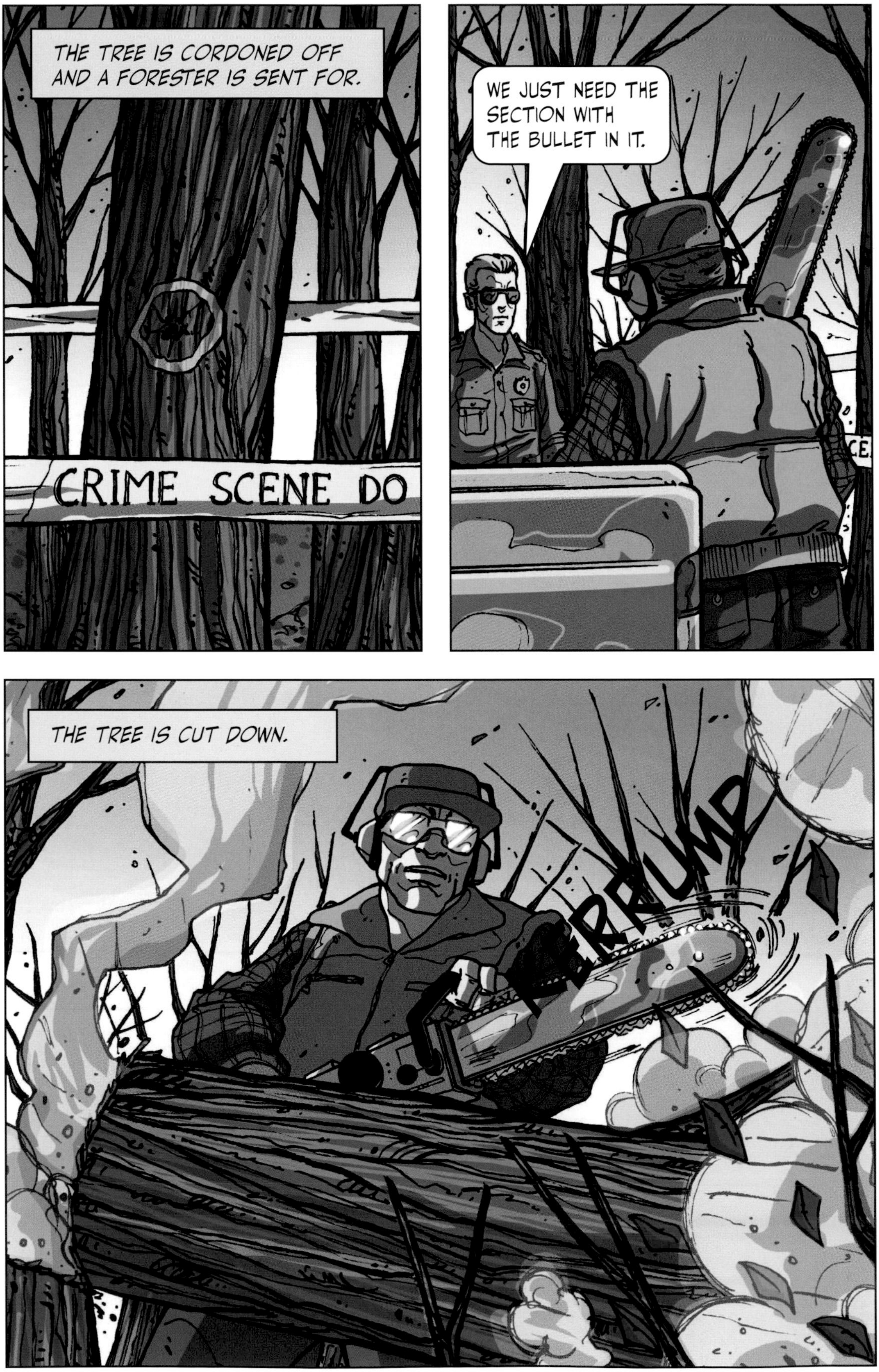

THE TREE IS CORDONED OFF AND A FORESTER IS SENT FOR.
CRIME SCENE DO
WE JUST NEED THE SECTION WITH THE BULLET IN IT.
THE TREE IS CUT DOWN.
KRRUMP

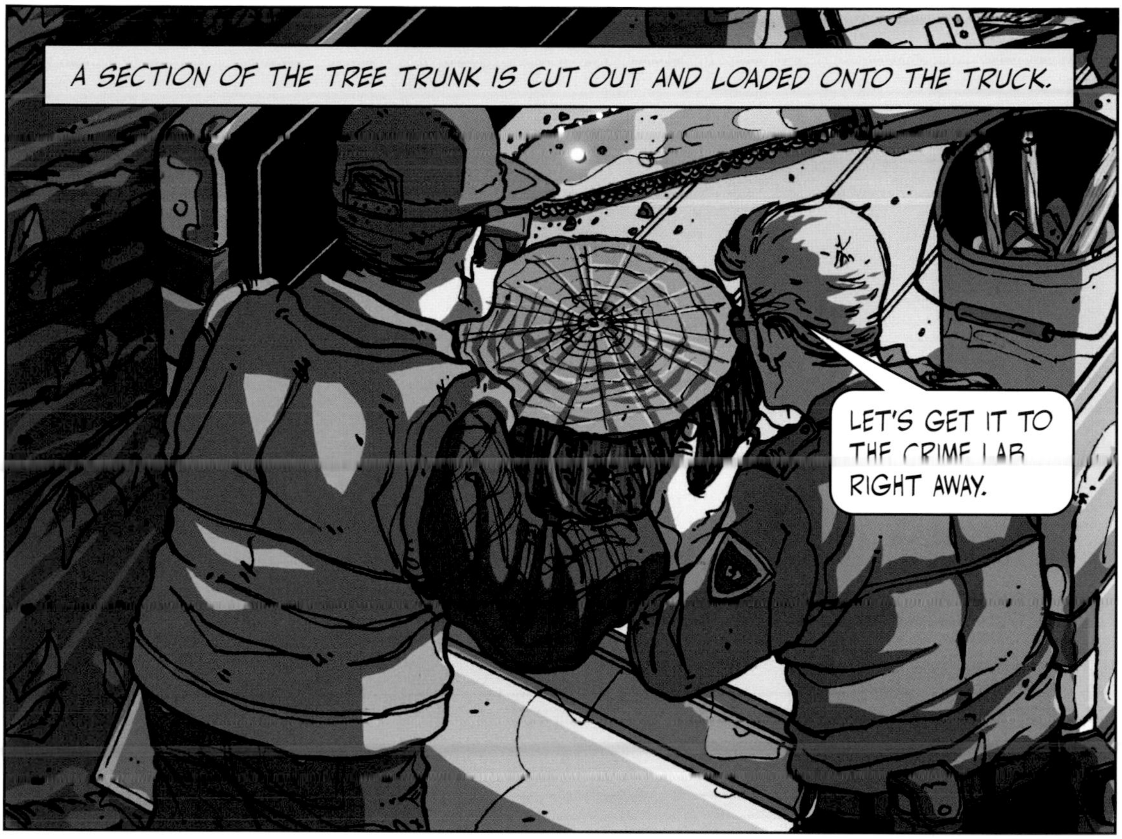
A SECTION OF THE TREE TRUNK IS CUT OUT AND LOADED ONTO THE TRUCK.
LET'S GET IT TO THE CRIME LAB RIGHT AWAY.

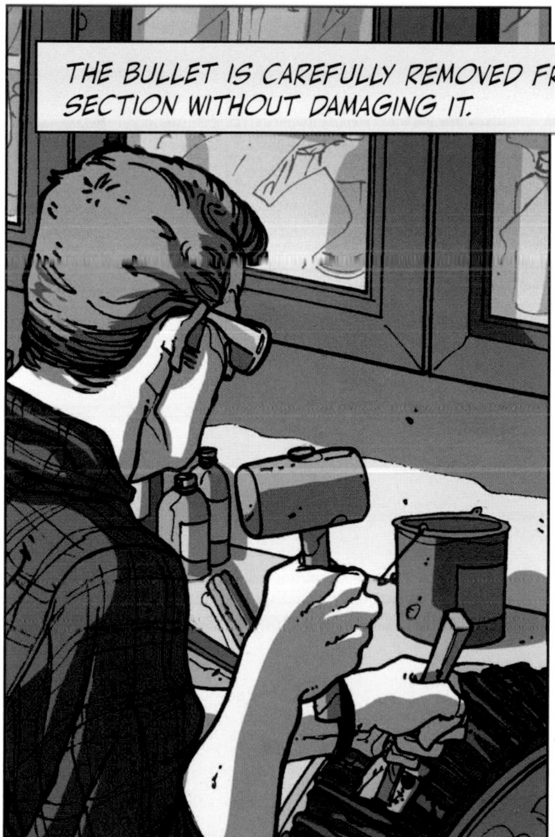
THE BULLET IS CAREFULLY REMOVED FROM THE TREE SECTION WITHOUT DAMAGING IT.

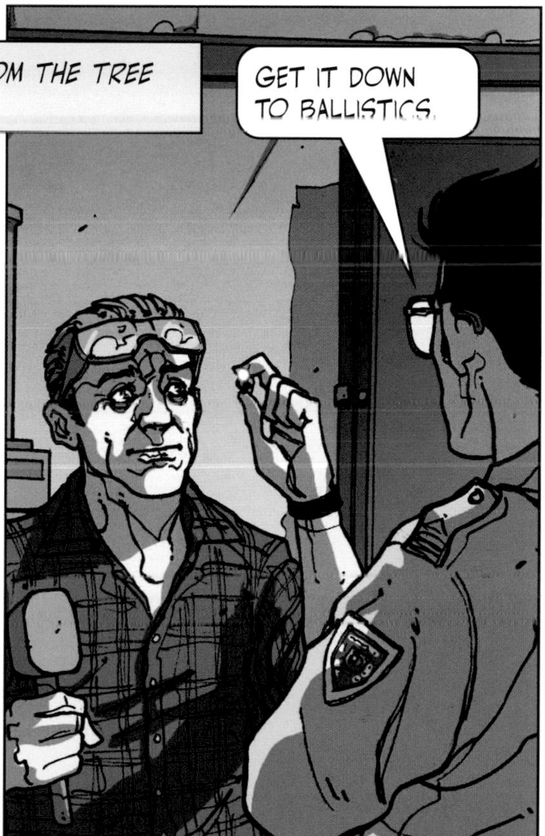
GET IT DOWN TO BALLISTICS.

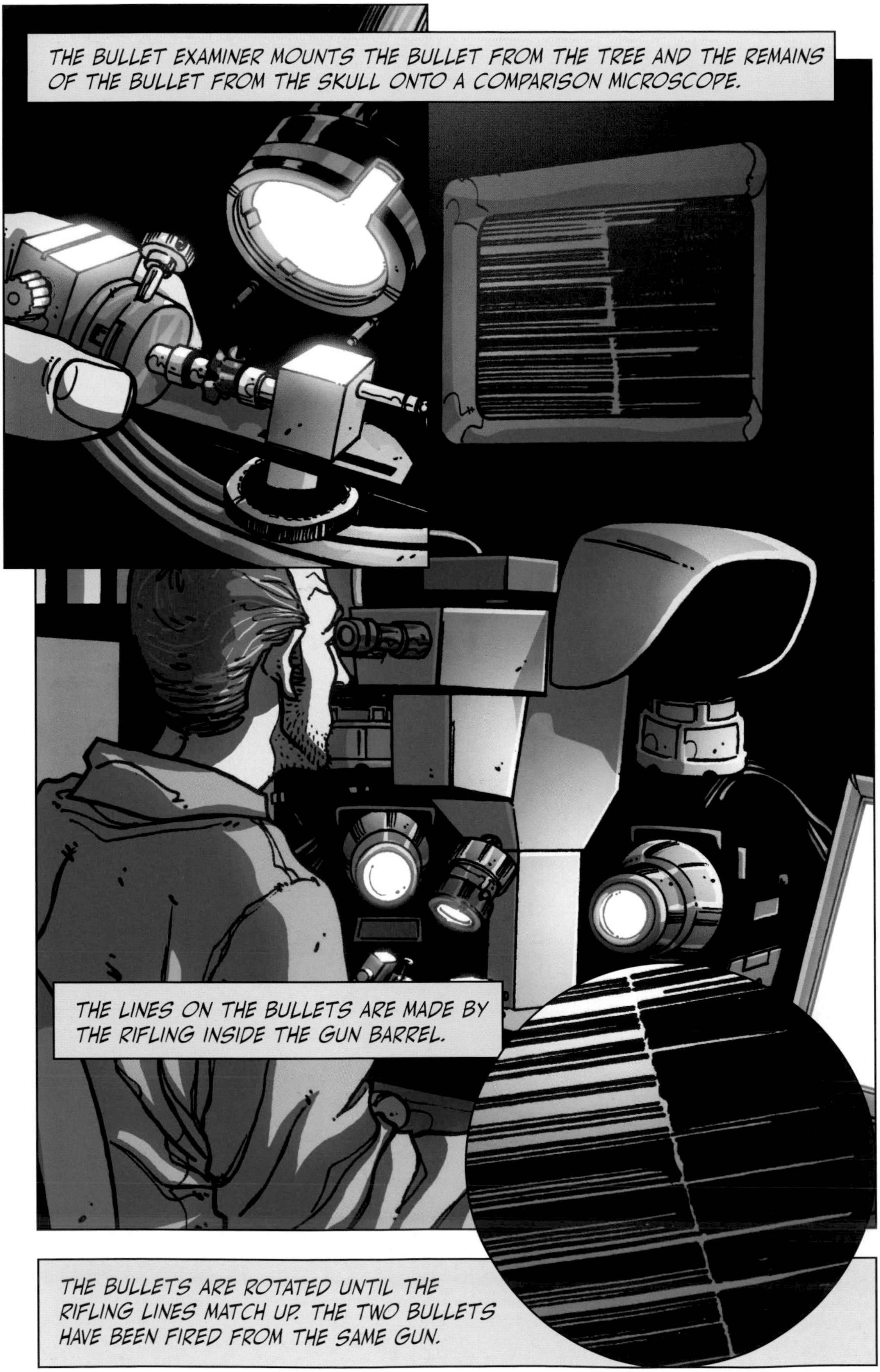
THE BULLET EXAMINER MOUNTS THE BULLET FROM THE TREE AND THE REMAINS OF THE BULLET FROM THE SKULL ONTO A COMPARISON MICROSCOPE.
THE LINES ON THE BULLETS ARE MADE BY THE RIFLING INSIDE THE GUN BARREL.
THE BULLETS ARE ROTATED UNTIL THE RIFLING LINES MATCH UP. THE TWO BULLETS HAVE BEEN FIRED FROM THE SAME GUN.

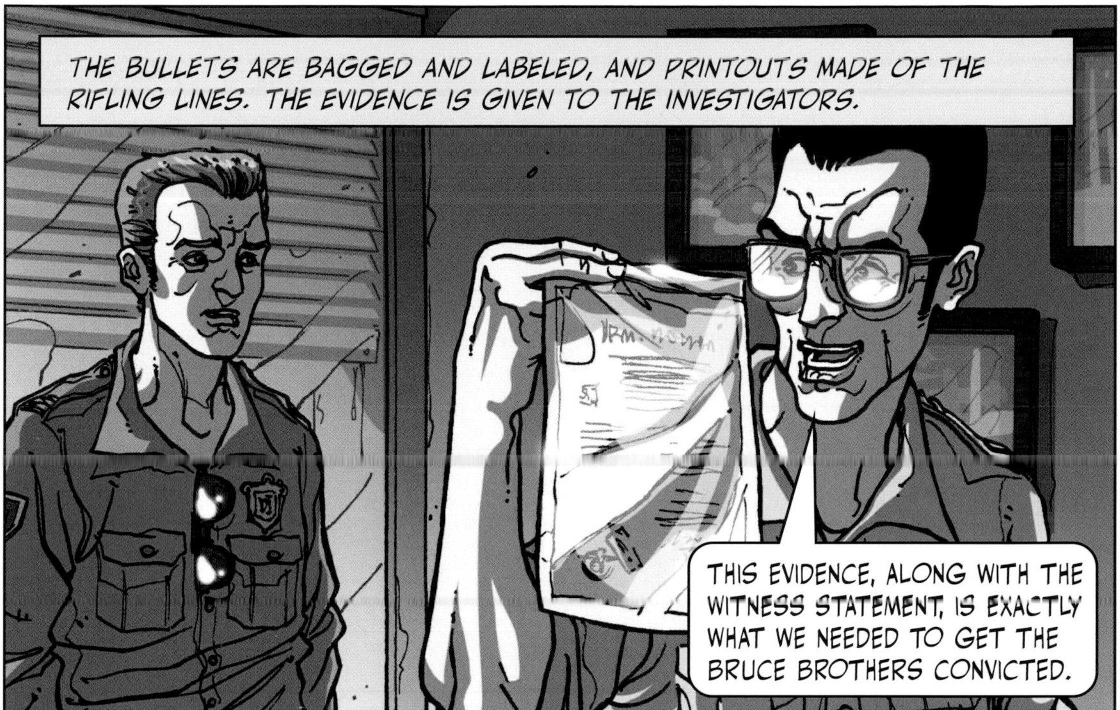
THE BULLETS ARE BAGGED AND LABELED, AND PRINTOUTS MADE OF THE RIFLING LINES. THE EVIDENCE IS GIVEN TO THE INVESTIGATORS.
THIS EVIDENCE, ALONG WITH THE WITNESS STATEMENT, IS EXACTLY WHAT WE NEEDED TO GET THE BRUCE BROTHERS CONVICTED.

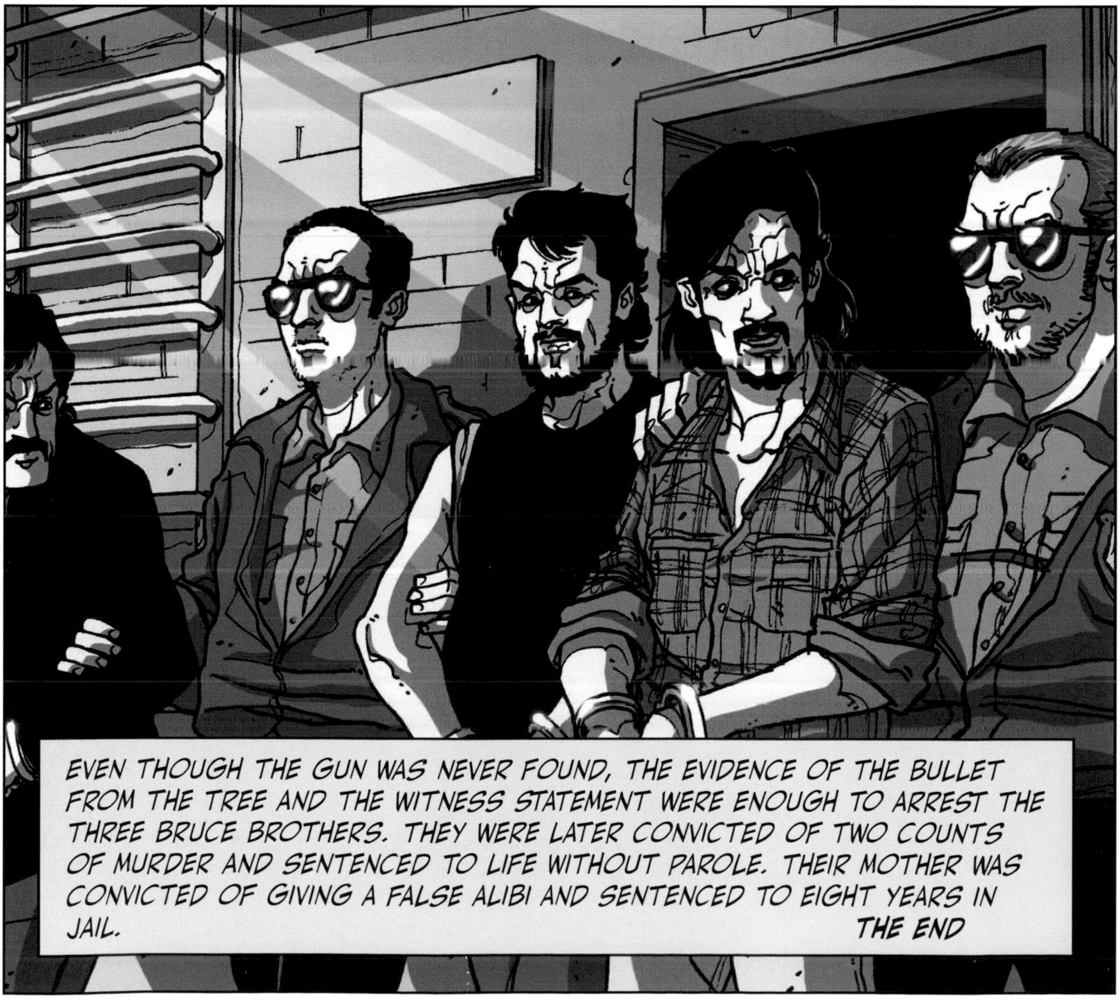
EVEN THOUGH THE GUN WAS NEVER FOUND, THE EVIDENCE OF THE BULLET FROM THE TREE AND THE WITNESS STATEMENT WERE ENOUGH TO ARREST THE THREE BRUCE BROTHERS. THEY WERE LATER CONVICTED OF TWO COUNTS OF MURDER AND SENTENCED TO LIFE WITHOUT PAROLE. THEIR MOTHER WAS CONVICTED OF GIVING A FALSE ALIBI AND SENTENCED TO EIGHT YEARS IN JAIL.
THE END

BULLET HOLES AND LASERS

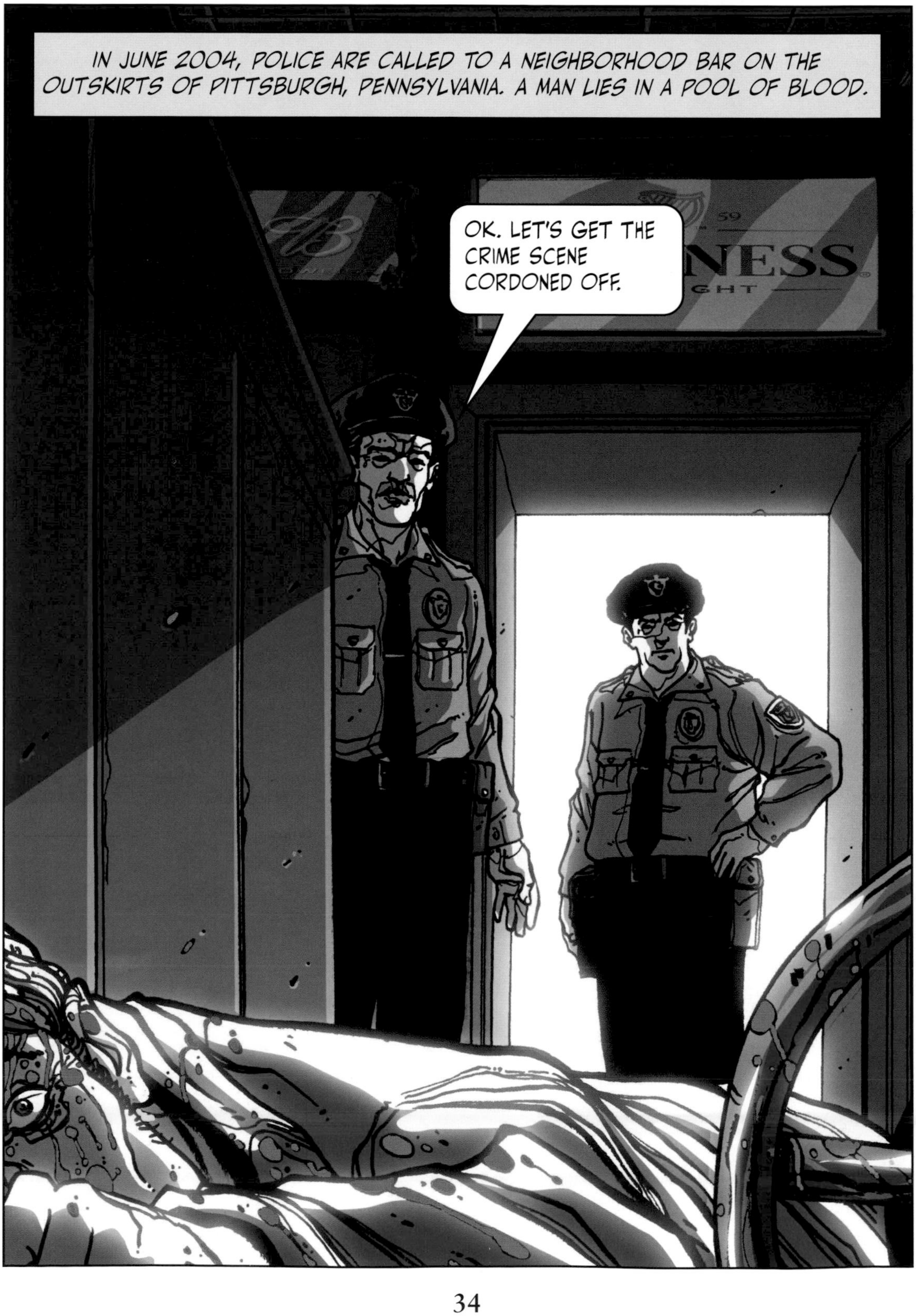
IN JUNE 2004, POLICE ARE CALLED TO A NEIGHBORHOOD BAR ON THE OUTSKIRTS OF PITTSBURGH, PENNSYLVANIA. A MAN LIES IN A POOL OF BLOOD.
OK. LET'S GET THE CRIME SCENE CORDONED OFF.

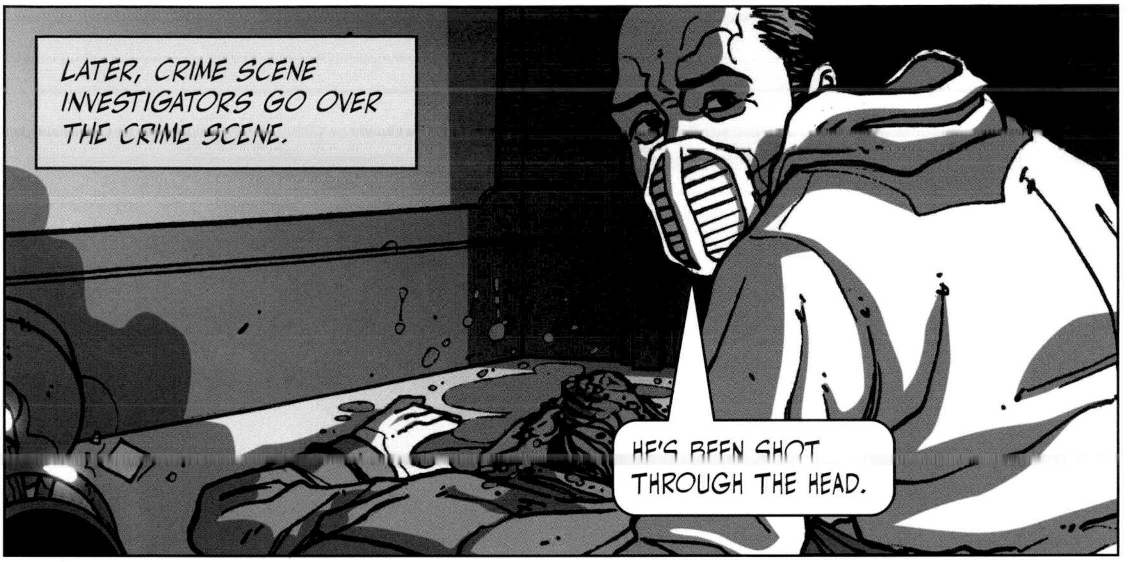
LATER, CRIME SCENE INVESTIGATORS GO OVER THE CRIME SCENE.
HE'S BEEN SHOT THROUGH THE HEAD.

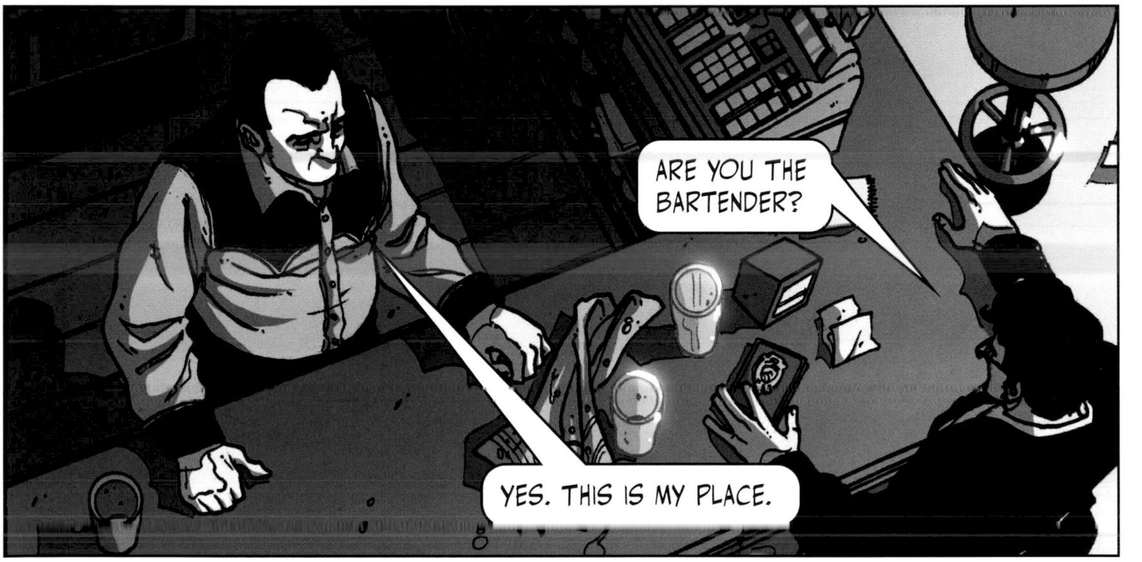
ARE YOU THE BARTENDER?
YES. THIS IS MY PLACE.

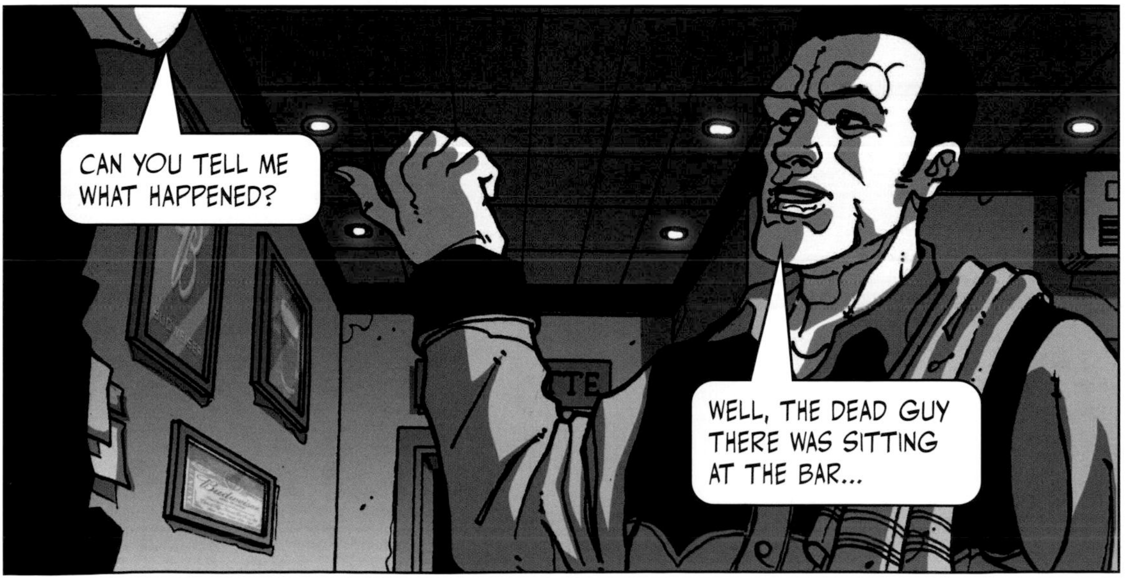
CAN YOU TELL ME WHAT HAPPENED?
WELL, THE DEAD GUY THERE WAS SITTING AT THE BAR...

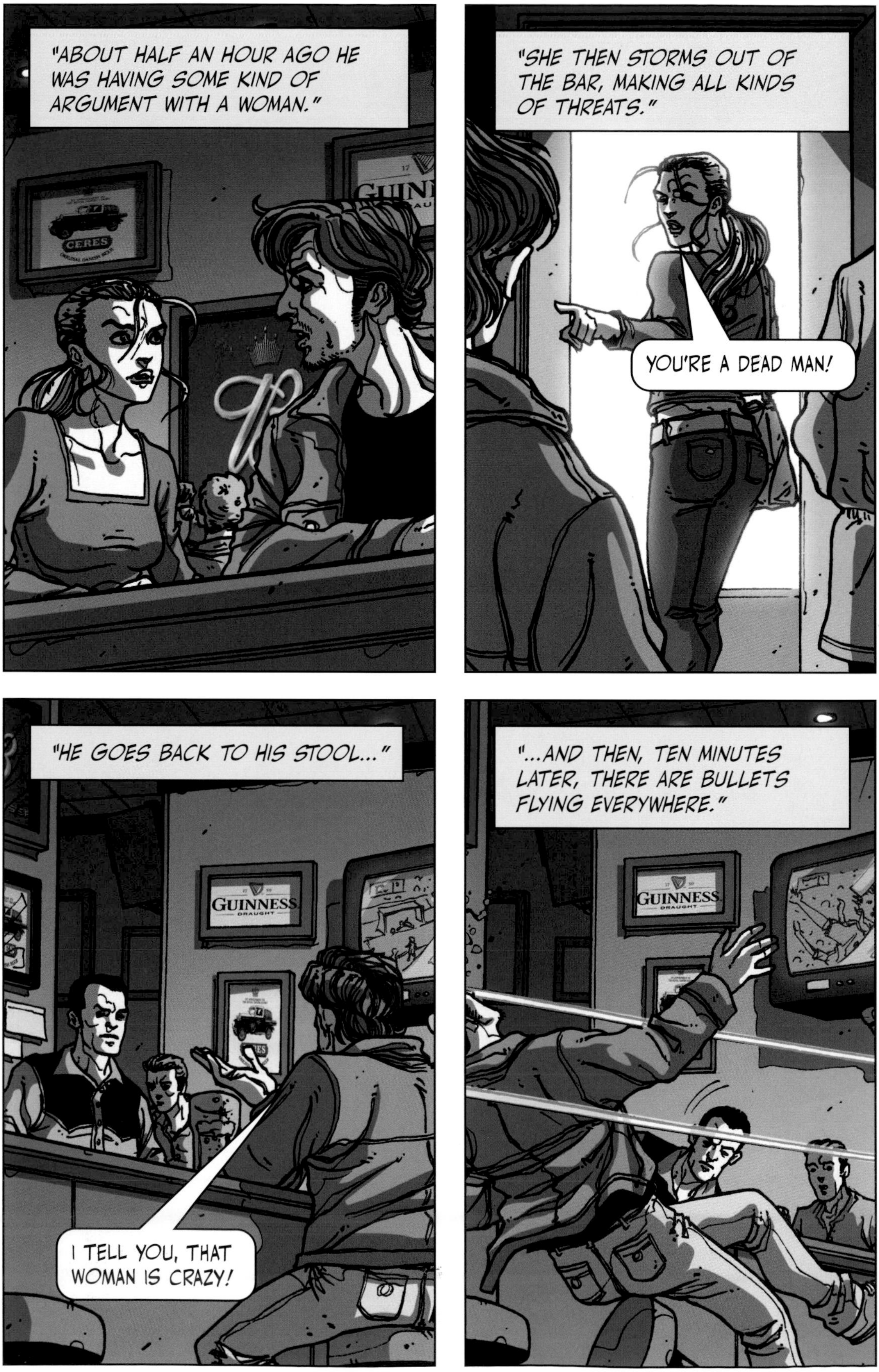
"ABOUT HALF AN HOUR AGO HE WAS HAVING SOME KIND OF ARGUMENT WITH A WOMAN."
CERES
"SHE THEN STORMS OUT OF THE BAR, MAKING ALL KINDS OF THREATS."
YOU'RE A DEAD MAN!
"HE GOES BACK TO HIS STOOL..."
GUINNESS
DRAUGHT
I TELL YOU, THAT WOMAN IS CRAZY!
"...AND THEN, TEN MINUTES LATER, THERE ARE BULLETS FLYING EVERYWHERE."
GUINNESS
DRAUGHT

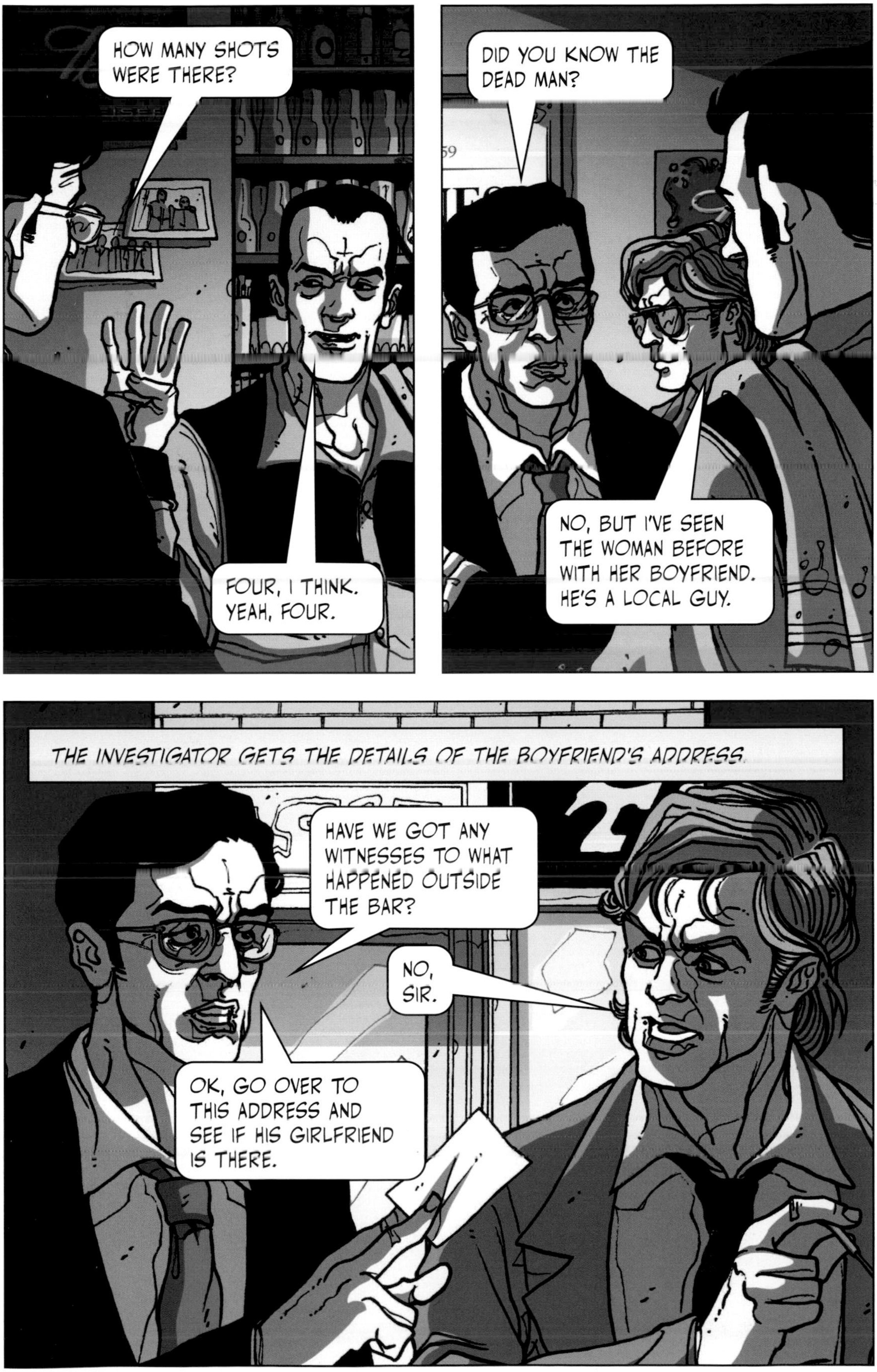
HOW MANY SHOTS WERE THERE?
FOUR, I THINK. YEAH, FOUR.
DID YOU KNOW THE DEAD MAN?
NO, BUT I'VE SEEN THE WOMAN BEFORE WITH HER BOYFRIEND. HE'S A LOCAL GUY.
THE INVESTIGATOR GETS THE DETAILS OF THE BOYFRIEND'S ADDRESS.
HAVE WE GOT ANY WITNESSES TO WHAT HAPPENED OUTSIDE THE BAR?
NO, SIR.
OK, GO OVER TO THIS ADDRESS AND SEE IF HIS GIRLFRIEND IS THERE.

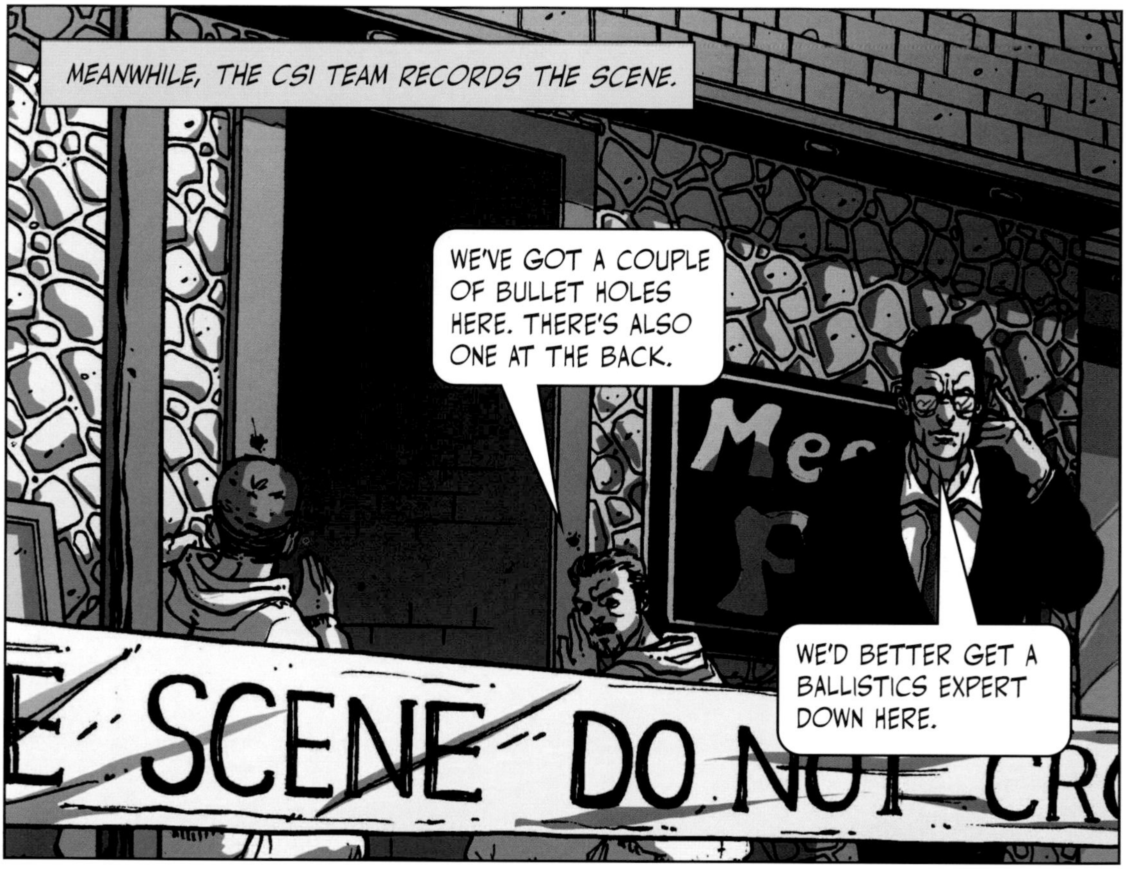
MEANWHILE, THE CSI TEAM RECORDS THE SCENE.
WE'VE GOT A COUPLE OF BULLET HOLES HERE. THERE'S ALSO ONE AT THE BACK.
WE'D BETTER GET A BALLISTICS EXPERT DOWN HERE.
SCENE DO NOT CRO

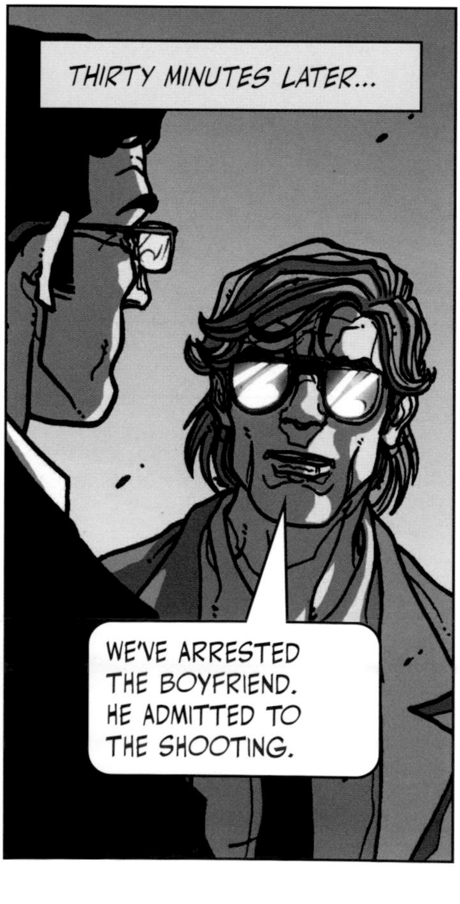
THIRTY MINUTES LATER...
WE'VE ARRESTED THE BOYFRIEND. HE ADMITTED TO THE SHOOTING.

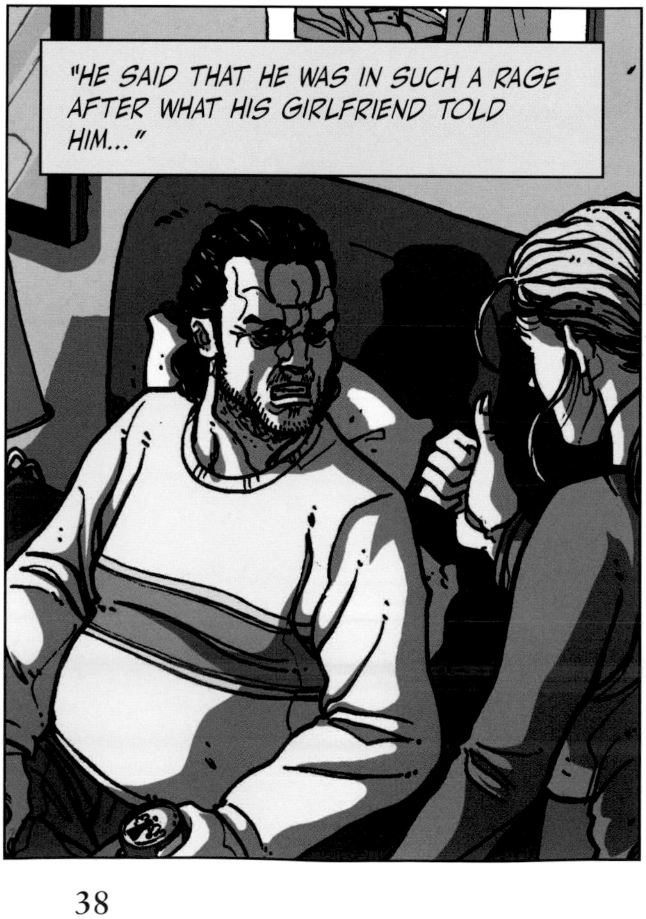
"HE SAID THAT HE WAS IN SUCH A RAGE AFTER WHAT HIS GIRLFRIEND TOLD HIM..."

"HE PICKED UP HIS THIRTY-EIGHT AND DROVE UP TO THE BAR."

"AS HE DROVE PAST, HE FIRED SOME SHOTS INTO THE BAR."

BLAM BLAM BLAM BLAM

THAT DOESN'T SOUND RIGHT. THAT'S A LUCKY SHOT FROM A MOVING VEHICLE.

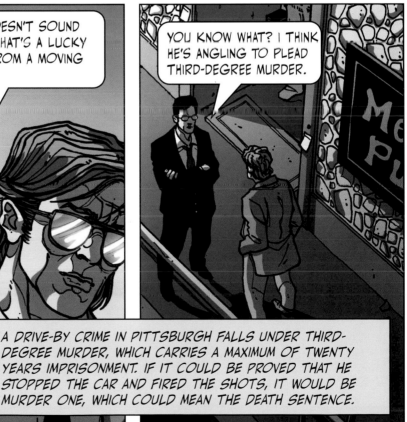

YOU KNOW WHAT? I THINK HE'S ANGLING TO PLEAD THIRD-DEGREE MURDER.

A DRIVE-BY CRIME IN PITTSBURGH FALLS UNDER THIRD-DEGREE MURDER, WHICH CARRIES A MAXIMUM OF TWENTY YEARS IMPRISONMENT. IF IT COULD BE PROVED THAT HE STOPPED THE CAR AND FIRED THE SHOTS, IT WOULD BE MURDER ONE, WHICH COULD MEAN THE DEATH SENTENCE.

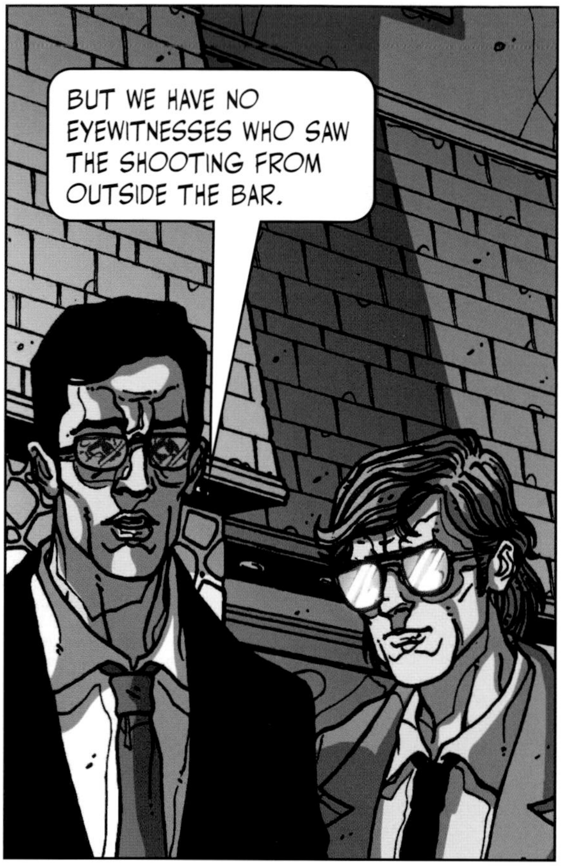
BUT WE HAVE NO EYEWITNESSES WHO SAW THE SHOOTING FROM OUTSIDE THE BAR.

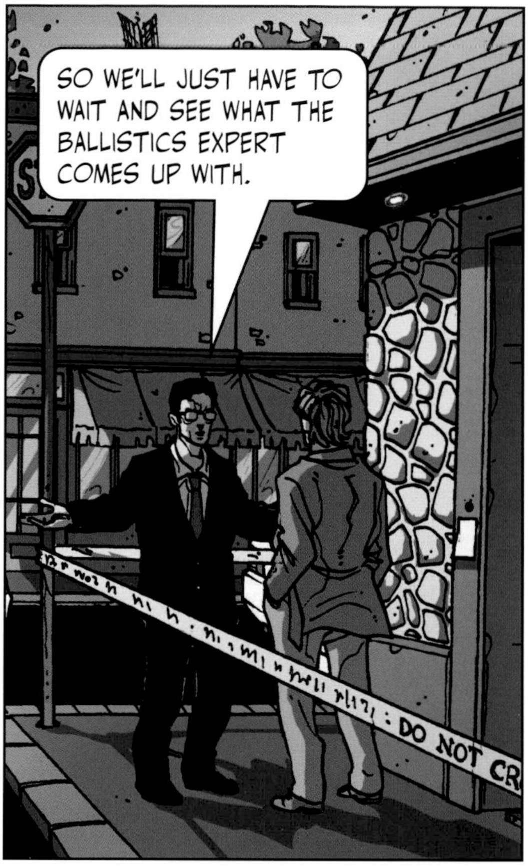
SO WE'LL JUST HAVE TO WAIT AND SEE WHAT THE BALLISTICS EXPERT COMES UP WITH.
DO NOT CR

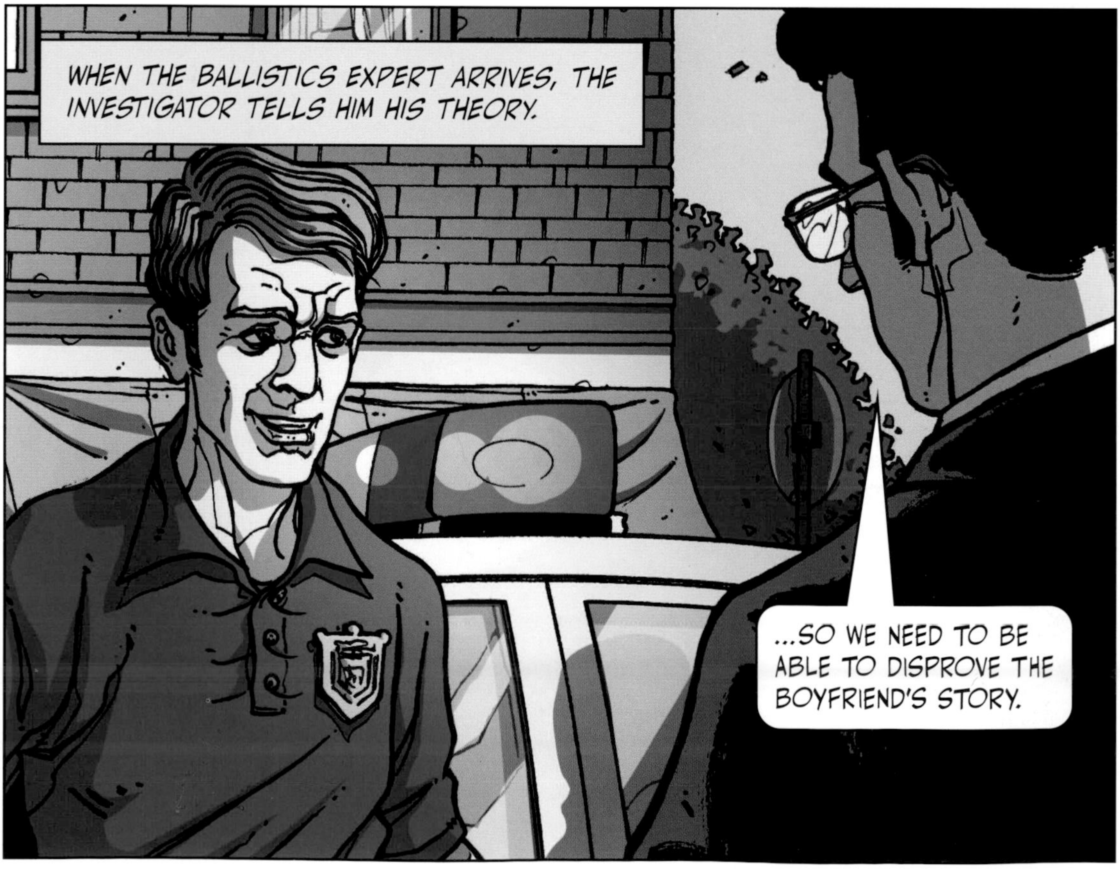
WHEN THE BALLISTICS EXPERT ARRIVES, THE INVESTIGATOR TELLS HIM HIS THEORY.
...SO WE NEED TO BE ABLE TO DISPROVE THE BOYFRIEND'S STORY.

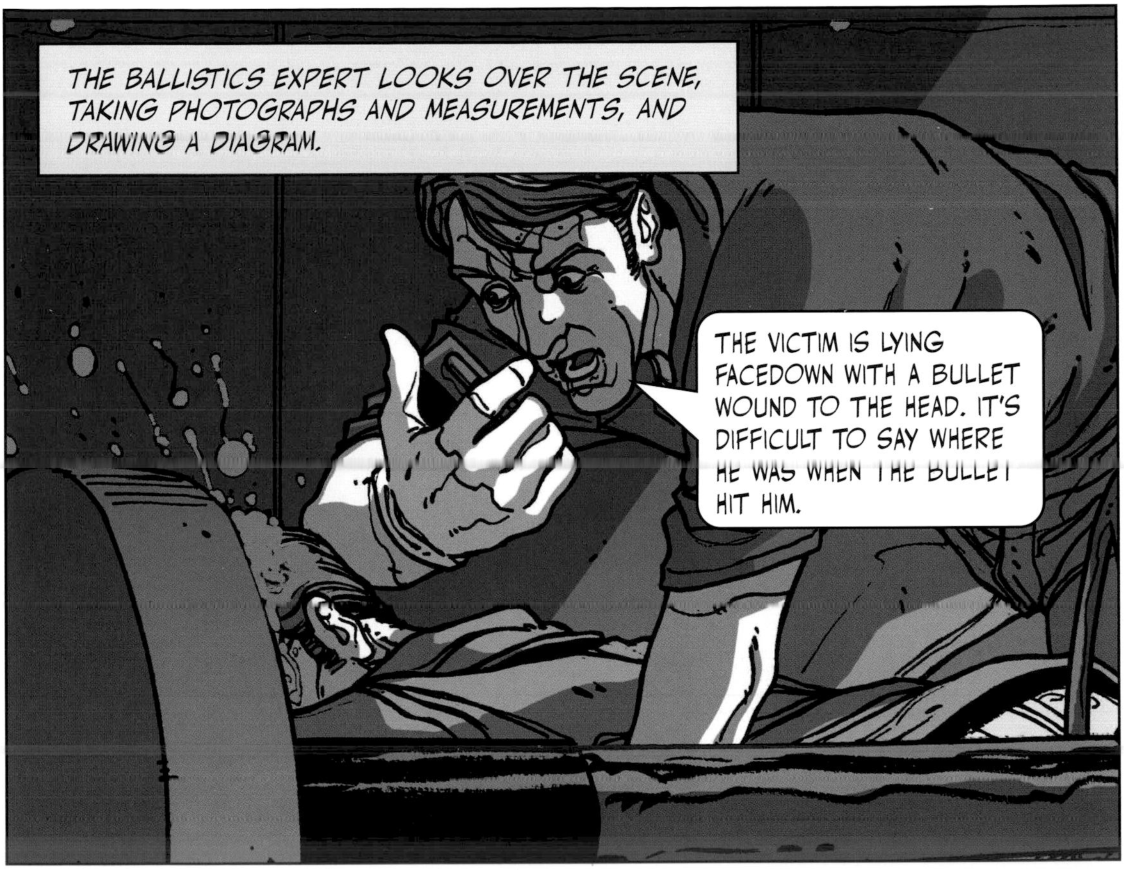
THE BALLISTICS EXPERT LOOKS OVER THE SCENE, TAKING PHOTOGRAPHS AND MEASUREMENTS, AND DRAWING A DIAGRAM.
THE VICTIM IS LYING FACEDOWN WITH A BULLET WOUND TO THE HEAD. IT'S DIFFICULT TO SAY WHERE HE WAS WHEN THE BULLET HIT HIM.

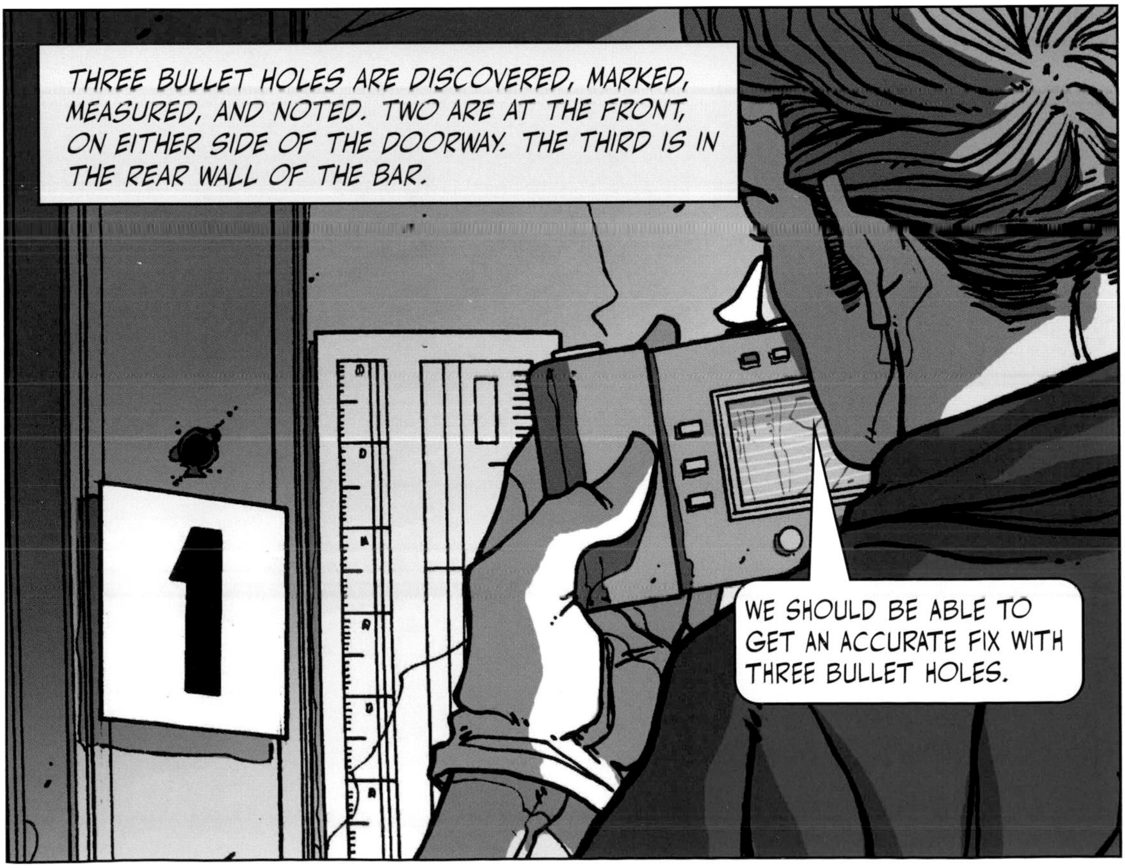
THREE BULLET HOLES ARE DISCOVERED, MARKED, MEASURED, AND NOTED. TWO ARE AT THE FRONT, ON EITHER SIDE OF THE DOORWAY. THE THIRD IS IN THE REAR WALL OF THE BAR.
1
WE SHOULD BE ABLE TO GET AN ACCURATE FIX WITH THREE BULLET HOLES.

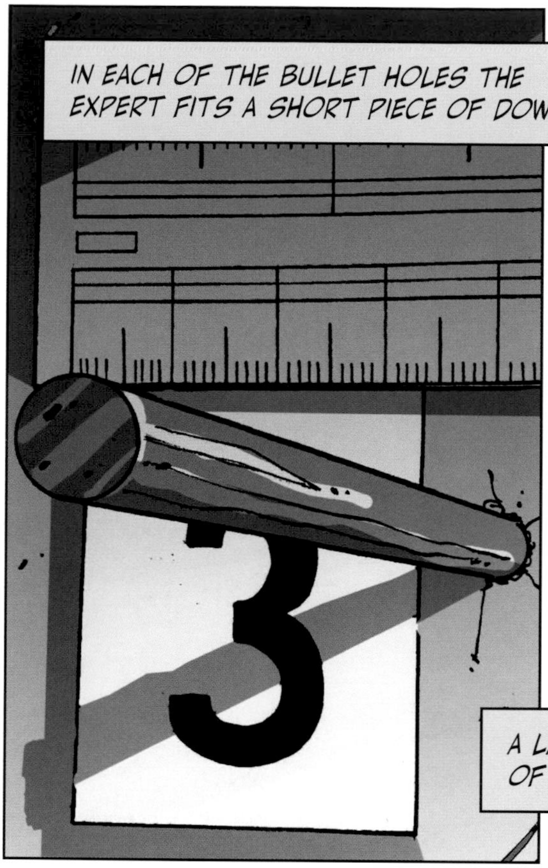
IN EACH OF THE BULLET HOLES THE EXPERT FITS A SHORT PIECE OF DOWEL.

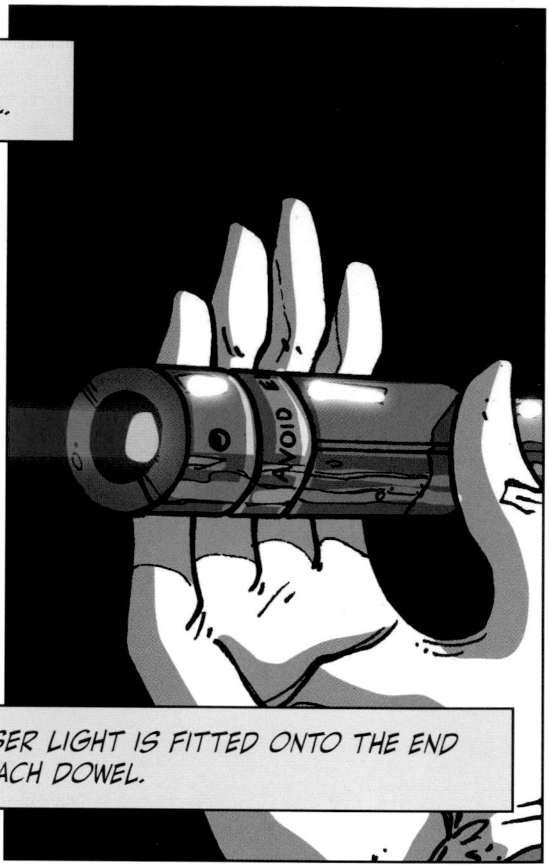
A LASER LIGHT IS FITTED ONTO THE END OF EACH DOWEL.

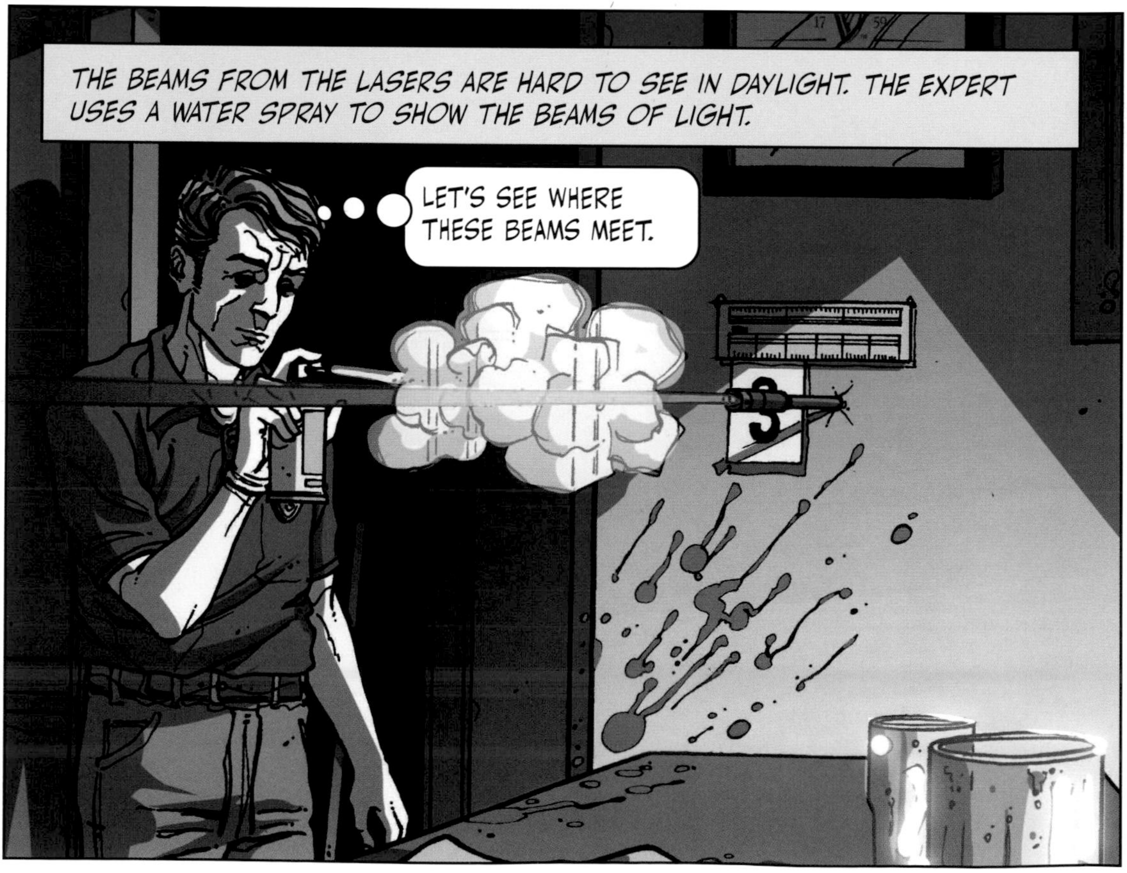
THE BEAMS FROM THE LASERS ARE HARD TO SEE IN DAYLIGHT. THE EXPERT USES A WATER SPRAY TO SHOW THE BEAMS OF LIGHT.
LET'S SEE WHERE THESE BEAMS MEET.

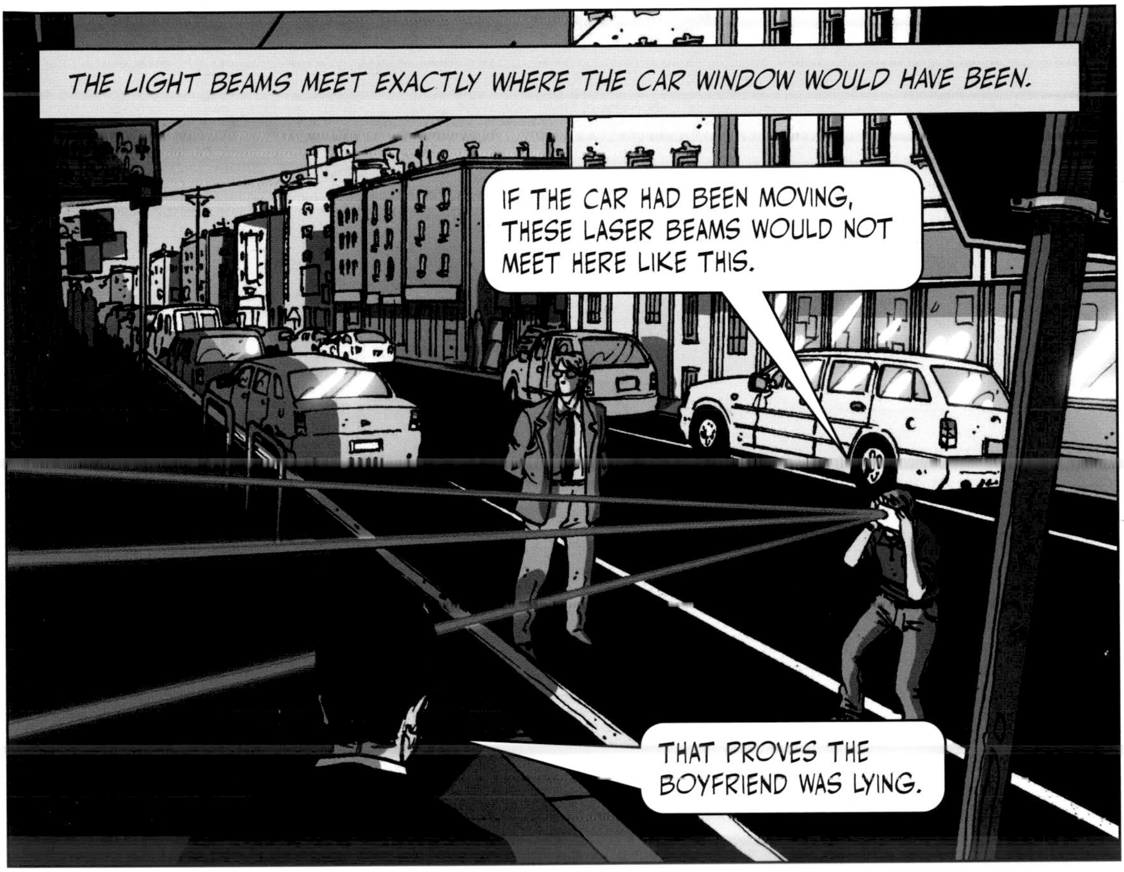
THE LIGHT BEAMS MEET EXACTLY WHERE THE CAR WINDOW WOULD HAVE BEEN.
IF THE CAR HAD BEEN MOVING, THESE LASER BEAMS WOULD NOT MEET HERE LIKE THIS.
THAT PROVES THE BOYFRIEND WAS LYING.

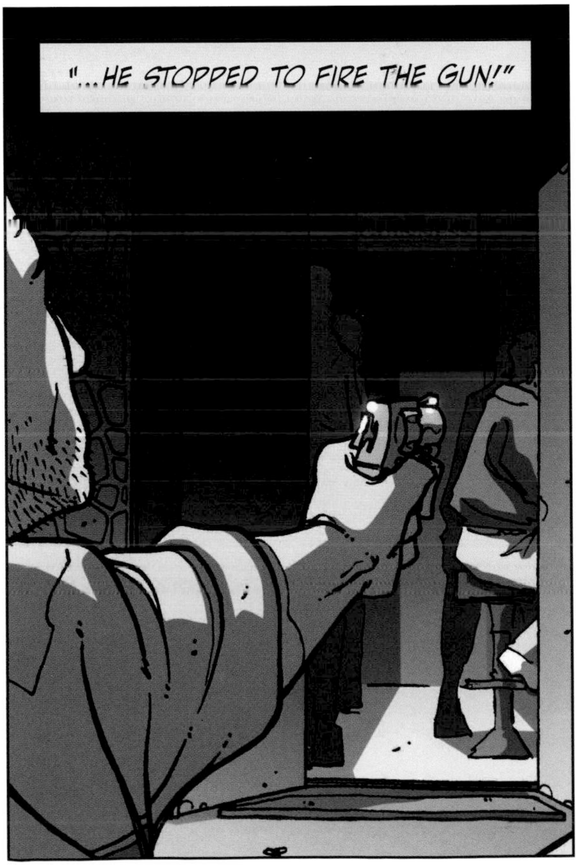
"...HE STOPPED TO FIRE THE GUN!"

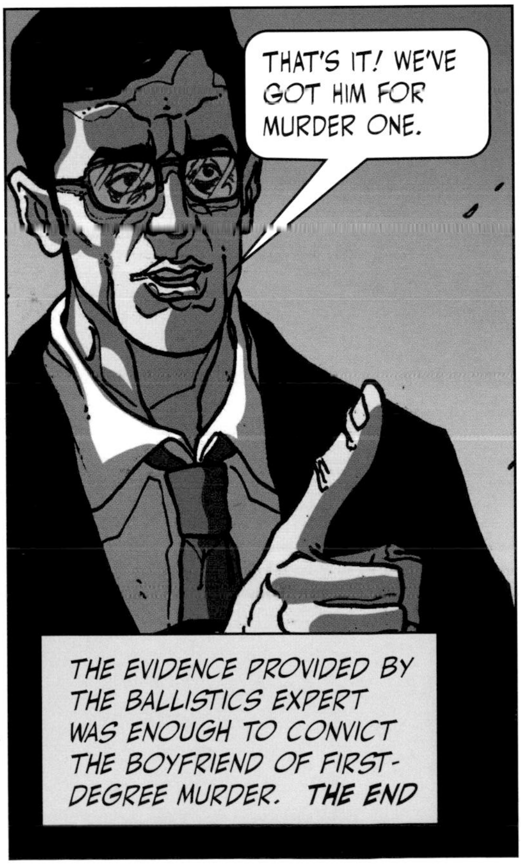
THAT'S IT! WE'VE GOT HIM FOR MURDER ONE.
THE EVIDENCE PROVIDED BY THE BALLISTICS EXPERT WAS ENOUGH TO CONVICT THE BOYFRIEND OF FIRST-DEGREE MURDER. THE END

OTHER FAMOUS CASES

The wars of the seventeenth century taught the working classes how to fire a gun, and the result was a sudden rise in gun-related crime. Early weapons were loaded by pouring gunpowder down the barrel, followed by a round bullet, and finally a wad of paper, which was rammed down the barrel to stop the bullet and gunpowder from falling out.

Thomas Richardson

In 1860, a police officer was shot in Lincolnshire, England, by Thomas Richardson, a suspected poacher. At the scene of the crime a piece of newspaper was found, which had been used as wadding. When the suspect's double-barreled gun was examined, wadding from the same newspaper was found in the undischarged barrel. Both had come from the same page of *The Times* newspaper. Richardson was convicted of murder and hanged.

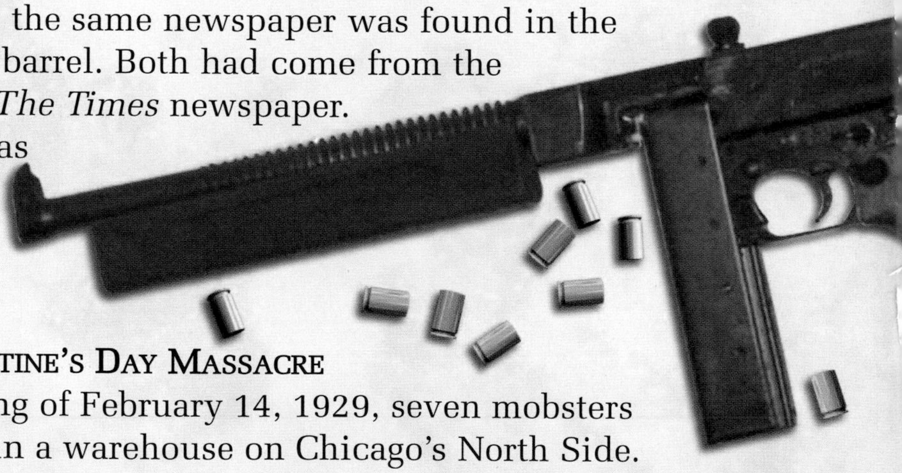

The St. Valentine's Day Massacre

On the morning of February 14, 1929, seven mobsters were waiting in a warehouse on Chicago's North Side. Five men, some dressed as policemen, arrived in a police car. They lined the mobsters against a wall and mowed them down with machine guns. The shooters left behind seventy cartridge cases, which were identified as coming from Thompson submachine guns. When it was suspected that the police were involved, Calvin Goddard was called in as an independent investigator. He fired all eight Thompson machine guns owned by the police and compared the cartridges with those from the crime scene. No matches were found. So the shooters had been impersonating police officers.

Ten months later, two Thompson machine guns were found at the home of a hit man for Al Capone. Goddard proved they were the guns used in the murders, and one of the killers was sent to prison. This case inspired two businessmen to set up the first independent crime lab in the country, at Northwestern University in Chicago.

The Bedouin Trackers and the Ballistics Examiner

In 1928, Sir Sydney Smith was working for the Egyptian government as the Principal Medico-Legal Expert to the Ministry of Justice. He was called in by the police to help investigate a murdered postman, found lying in the desert. The post-mortem had revealed that the victim had been shot through the head by a .303 rifle but the bullet had not been found. The police, who could find no traces left by the murderer, had called in Bedouin trackers. They immediately found tracks of footprints leading to where the victim had been lying. Tracing them back, they found the place where the murderer had fired the weapon and discovered an empty .303 rifle cartridge. The murderer had fired the shot, walked to the victim to see that he was dead, and then left the scene. The Bedouin were able to follow his tracks to a fort, where six soldiers were stationed. The next day all six soldiers were made to walk across a stretch of sand several times. Each time this was done the Bedouin trackers identified the footprints of one man. Meanwhile, Smith had the soldiers' six rifles fired and compared the empty cartridges to the one found at the crime scene. One cartridge matched exactly and it belonged to the same man the Bedouin had picked out. The man was arrested and later proved guilty of the crime.

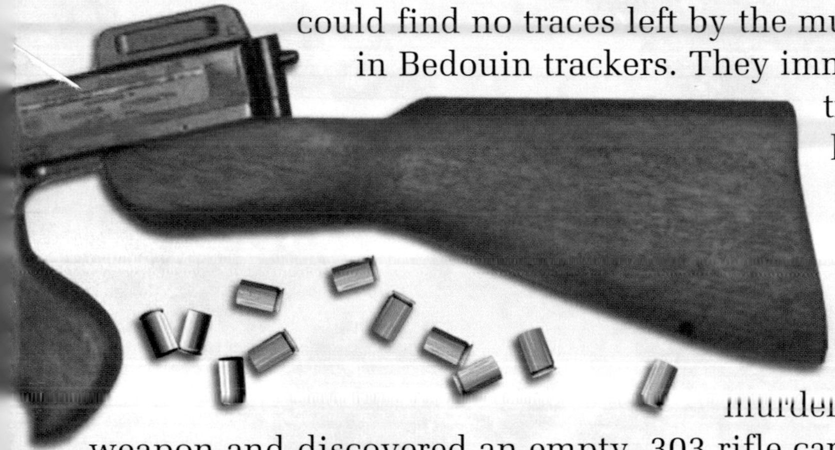

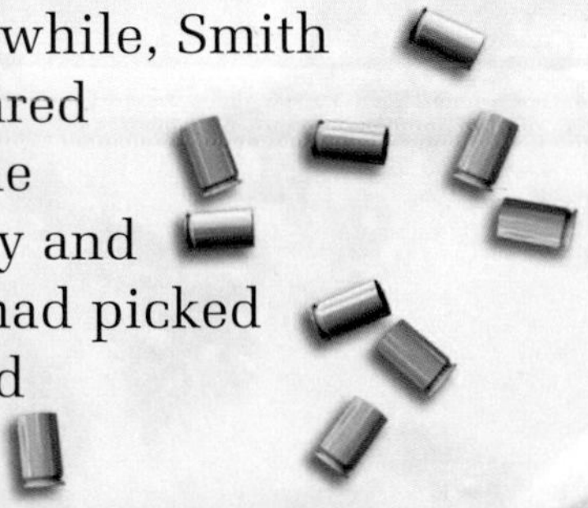

GLOSSARY

alibi An account of where a person was when a crime was committed, usually proved by other people.

archive A collection of documents or records held in a place or on computers.

arson A criminal act of deliberately setting fire to a building.

attorney A lawyer.

breechblock A metal block in breech-loading firearms that is withdrawn to insert a cartridge and replaced to close the breech before firing.

bull's-eye lantern An early type of flashlight that had a single lens to focus a beam of light. The source of the light was a candle.

cartridge case The casing, usually made of brass, that holds the gunpowder and bullet of a firearm.

catalog A complete list of items, or to make a complete list of items.

confess To admit to a crime.

convict To find someone guilty in a trial by jury.

cordon off To close off an area with tape to prevent access.

dowel A thin, straight, wooden stick.

evidence A collection of items, witnesses, and information that supports a given fact in a court of law.

firearm A portable gun such as a rifle or pistol.

forensic anthropologist An expert who examines skeletal, badly decomposed, or otherwise unidentified human remains.

forester A person who manages and cares for trees.

investigate To carry out a detailed search for the facts and information about an incident in order to discover the truth.

loot Stolen money or valuables.

poacher A person who hunts for game or fishes illegally.

suspicious Showing caution or mistrust of something or someone.

undischarged Describing a weapon or piece of ammunition that has not been fired.

FOR MORE INFORMATION

ORGANIZATIONS

International Center for Scientific Research (CIRS)
B.P. 53
75222 Paris cedex 05
France
Web site: http://www.cirs-tm.org

National Forensic Science Technology Center
7881 114th Avenue North
Largo, FL 33773
(727) 549 6067
Web site: http://www.nfstc.org

FOR FURTHER READING

Frith, Alex. *Forensic Science*. London, England: Usborne Publishing Ltd., 2007.

Harvey, Gill. *True Stories of Crime and Detection*. London, England: Usborne Publishing Ltd., 2007.

Joyce, Jaime. *Bullet Proof!: The Evidence that Guns Leave Behind*. (24/7: Science Behind the Scenes: Forensic Files). London, England: Franklin Watts, 2007.

Pentland, Peter, and Pennie Stoyles. *Forensic Science*. New York, NY: Chelsea House Publishers, 2002.

Rainis, Kenneth, G. *Crime-Solving Science Projects: Forensic Science Experiments*. Berkeley Heights, NJ: Enslow Publishers, 2000.

Rollins, Barbara B., and Michael Dahl. *Ballistics*. Mankato, MN: Capstone Press, 2004.

INDEX

Web Sites

Due to the changing nature of Internet links, Rosen Publishing has developed an online list of Web sites related to the subject of this book. This site is updated regularly. Please use this link to access the list:

http://www.rosenlinks.com/gfs/dwwb